P9-ELT-361

Praise for *Become the Real Deal*

"In choosing whom to *willingly* follow, it often comes down to 'know, like, and trust.' And, each of these will occur to the degree people sense—rather, they *know*—that the person they experience is the real you; the authentic you. In other words, that you are in fact . . . The Real Deal! The good news is that this is already inside of you. The even better news is that you are about to learn from the master in her field how to tap into this sense of authenticity and communicate it much more effectively. The result will be more self-confidence, more effectiveness, and a true connection with those you wish to connect. Make a study of these teachings and enjoy the accelerated growth you'll experience both personally and professionally. Great job, Connie. Terrific!!"

—**Bob Burg**, *Wall Street Journal* and *BusinessWeek* Bestselling Coauthor of *The Go-Giver* and *Go Givers Sell More*

"If you are looking to earn trust and build influence with others, realness is a must. Read *Become the Real Deal* to learn how to make that a part of your professional fabric."

—**Tim Sanders**, *New York Times* Bestselling author of *Love Is the Killer App: How To Win Business and Influence Friends*

"*Become the Real Deal* is a masterful guide to harnessing your natural abilities to influence others, radiate executive presence, and build the lifelong relationships you need to succeed."

—**Andrew Sobel**, *Wall Street Journal* Bestselling Author of *Power Questions* and *Clients for Life*

"All leaders need to be *the real deal* and in this insightful and useful new book you get field-tested strategies—and important warnings—to make sure you *Become the Real Deal*. Whether you want to advance your career or move your team to take action, executive coach Connie Dieken reveals the layers that will help you master your presence and influence."

—**Mark Sanborn**, *New York Times* and *Wall Street Journal* Bestselling Author of *The Fred Factor* and *Fred 2.0*

"Authenticity is the foundation of great leadership, so, as leaders, we need to be ourselves every day, in everything we do. Connie Dieken artfully identifies the situations and relationships that push us off center, and then she pulls us right back to the core of who we really are. *Become the Real Deal* is . . . well . . . the real deal."

—**Steve Farber**, *New York Times* Bestselling Author of *The Radical Leap Re-Energized* and *Greater Than Yourself*

"A fascinating read, Connie Dieken's insightful research and strategies will help you center yourself, engage others, and boost your leadership gravitas."

—**Sally Hogshead**, Hall of Fame Speaker, CEO and Founder of The Fascination Advantage

"Connie Dieken is a master of influence and communication. Her book *Become the Real Deal* is the real deal. Get it. Devour it."

—**Randy Gage**, *New York Times* Bestselling Author of *Risky Is the New Safe*

"Today's leaders are called to be authentic and perfect at the same time. It's an impossible standard, but Connie Dieken's new book will show you how to thread this new leadership needle to achieve both inner and outer presence. It's a must-read."

—**Nick Morgan**, Author of *Trust Me*

"Authenticity is today's must-have leadership trait. Connie Dieken's three-layered approach will help you balance *being* with *doing* to increase your influence and become the *Real Deal*."

—**Carol Roth**, WGN Radio Host, and *New York Times* Bestselling Author of *The Entrepreneur Equation*

"If you're looking to influence boldly, earn trust, and become a leadership powerhouse, *Become the Real Deal* is for you. Connie Dieken is a powerful, fresh voice in leadership presence. "

—**Michael Port**, *New York Times* Bestselling Author of *Book Yourself Solid* and *The Think Big Manifesto*

"I've been an ardent fan and follower of Connie Dieken's brilliance for years. I listen to what Connie says and read what Connie writes and try as hard as possible to apply her insight and output to my activities and my life. Connie has changed the way I look at myself and the way I present myself to the world. What she tells me simply makes sense. Better yet—it works."

—**Bruce Turkel**, Author of *Building Brand Value*

"I place a premium on amazing experiences. As you dive into Connie's *Become the Real Deal*, you'll discover compelling stories and remarkable guidance on how to transform your leadership approach. You may not want to come up for air until you finish."

—**Shep Hyken**, *New York Times* and *Wall Street Journal* Bestselling Author of *The Amazement Revolution*

BECOME THE
REAL DEAL

The Proven Path to Influence and
Executive Presence

CONNIE
DIEKEN

WILEY

Cover design: Wiley

Copyright © 2013 by Connie Dieken. All rights reserved.

Published by John Wiley & Sons, Inc., Hoboken, New Jersey.

Published simultaneously in Canada.

No part of this publication may be reproduced, stored in a retrieval system, or transmitted in any form or by any means, electronic, mechanical, photocopying, recording, scanning, or otherwise, except as permitted under Section 107 or 108 of the 1976 United States Copyright Act, without either the prior written permission of the Publisher, or authorization through payment of the appropriate per-copy fee to the Copyright Clearance Center, 222 Rosewood Drive, Danvers, MA 01923, (978) 750-8400, fax (978) 646-8600, or on the web at www.copyright.com. Requests to the Publisher for permission should be addressed to the Permissions Department, John Wiley & Sons, Inc., 111 River Street, Hoboken, NJ 07030, (201) 748-6011, fax (201) 748-6008, or online at www.wiley.com/go/permissions.

Limit of Liability/Disclaimer of Warranty: While the publisher and author have used their best efforts in preparing this book, they make no representations or warranties with the respect to the accuracy or completeness of the contents of this book and specifically disclaim any implied warranties of merchantability or fitness for a particular purpose. No warranty may be created or extended by sales representatives or written sales materials. The advice and strategies contained herein may not be suitable for your situation. You should consult with a professional where appropriate. Neither the publisher nor the author shall be liable for damages arising herefrom.

For general information about our other products and services, please contact our Customer Care Department within the United States at (800) 762-2974, outside the United States at (317) 572-3993 or fax (317) 572-4002.

Wiley publishes in a variety of print and electronic formats and by print-on-demand. Some material included with standard print versions of this book may not be included in e-books or in print-on-demand. If this book refers to media such as a CD or DVD that is not included in the version you purchased, you may download this material at http://booksupport.wiley.com. For more information about Wiley products, visit www.wiley.com.

Library of Congress Cataloging-in-Publication Data:

Dieken, Connie, 1959-
  Become the real deal : the proven path to influence & executive presence / Connie Dieken.
      pages cm
  Includes index.
  ISBN 978-1-118-63378-6 (cloth); ISBN 978-1-118-75510-5 (ebk);
  ISBN 978-1-118-75505-1 (ebk); ISBN 978-1-118-75512-9 (ebk)
  1. Executive ability. 2. Executives. 3. Influence (Psychology) 4. Leadership. I. Title.
  HD38.2.D54 2013
  658.4'09–dc23
                                                                                        2013017388

Printed in the United States of America

10 9 8 7 6 5 4 3 2 1

To Joan

Scholar. Nurse. Wife. Single mother.
Sunday school teacher. Girl Scout leader.

Cancer survivor. Cancer victim.

Thank you for modeling the real deal, mom, no
matter what hand life dealt you. Your presence lives
on in your children, grandchildren, and the countless
lives that you influenced.

Contents

viii   *Contents*

Foreword

Connie Dieken's *Become the Real Deal* strikes a chord with me. She says, "The world demands perfection, yet craves authenticity." This is a challenge for many leaders. It's a challenge of identity and reputation, which I discuss extensively in my book *Mojo*.

Identity, or who you think you are, is subtle. Most people will answer this question based on others' perceptions of them. For example, they will respond, "I think people perceive me as someone who . . ." I stop them when they start with this answer, and tell them to take everyone else in the world out of the equation, including their spouse, family, and closest friends, and ask them to consider how they perceive *themselves*. Often this question is followed by a long period of silence as they struggle to get their own self-image into focus. This is very telling, because without a firm handle on our identity, we may never be able to be our true and authentic selves.

Reputation, or who other people think you are and what other people think you've done lately, are less subtle than the question about identity. Your reputation is a scoreboard that is kept by others. It's your coworkers, customers, friends, and sometimes even strangers, grabbing the right to grade your performance—and tell the rest of the world what they think about you! Although you can't be in total control of your reputation, you can maintain

Your reputation is your scoreboard

and improve it, and this can have an enormous impact on your ability to be "the real deal."

A leadership model to succeed

Connie takes the idea of being authentic—of having authenticity be part of our identity and also part of how others know us or our reputation—and gives us a solution to achieving it based on what she calls the Three Layers of Presence. Connie's layers are a wonderful leadership model that will help you as a leader succeed and lead at the highest levels. Thank you, Connie, for providing us with a model of leadership that will help us discover our true selves and our authenticity, and for giving us a solution to staying centered and "real" in the fast-paced world of business today!

Life is good.

—**Marshall Goldsmith,**
Author of the *New York Times*
Bestsellers *Mojo* and
What Got You Here Won't Get You There

Real Deal

Introduction

What Is the Real Deal?

"Just be yourself."

As a piece of advice, it's common—even clichéd. But it's far more demanding than it sounds, isn't it? Every day, you're flooded with stories and images of people whose personal qualities you may admire and want to emulate.

Haven't you secretly wondered if just being yourself is really enough? After all, to succeed in a competitive world, you need to measure up to some pretty high standards.

"Be yourself," you've been told. But while you're at it, be as visionary as Apple cofounder Steve Jobs. As hard-charging as Yahoo! CEO Marissa Mayer. As courageous as Nelson Mandela. As financially savvy as Warren Buffett. As athletic as LeBron James. As intuitive as Oprah Winfrey. As effortlessly beautiful as Halle Berry. As prescient as fashion mogul Michael Kors.

Just be yourself is incomplete advice

1

"Be yourself," the world tells you. But this tidy little tidbit is woefully incomplete advice. "Be yourself, *but measure up*," is what the world is *really* telling you if you want to reach your highest potential.

The missing chunk is how you get there

If you're a leader, you're on the receiving end of relentless and often conflicting advice about how to present yourself to the world. Perhaps you're urged to be active on social media in order to stay visible and to engage others. But what if you're naturally private? Maybe you've been prodded to display your vulnerable side in the conference room so that your staff will find you relatable. But what if you feel that exposing your personal experiences leaves you susceptible to career-limiting rumors—or even a leadership coup?

"Just be yourself" is well-meaning but inadequate guidance. It begs for more substance and measurement.

Over the past decade, I've been privileged to work with senior executives at some of the world's biggest corporations. These leaders, whose massive corner offices are often perched 50 stories above the concrete jungle below, appear poised, all-knowing, untouchable. And some of them are.

But the truth is, many executives fear that they're falling short of their full potential, and they worry about how they come across to others. That's where executive coaches like me come in: Our role is to help them reach their performance goals and motivate others while conquering the paradox of twenty-first-century leadership:

The world demands perfection, yet craves authenticity.

Think about the paradoxes in your life. You want to exude executive presence—yet still be genuine. You want to hone your speaking and influence skills—but not appear manipulative. You want to inspire top performance from others—yet not drive away top talent with your demands.

You want to be—*and to be seen as*—the real deal.

How do you balance the polarities of *perfection* and *authenticity* to lead at your peak level?

Like the rest of us, the super achievers I work with every day feel that the pressures of society and their work are constantly knocking them off-center. I've written this book to help anyone—from senior leader to junior hopeful—stay centered and be the real deal, using the lessons I've learned in boardrooms and conference rooms around the globe.

In today's hyperconnected, social-media–fueled world, public figures are immediately mocked for any perceived mistake or slip-up. Society tends to tear down anyone who seems *too* perfect. The truth, of course, is that we're all human—so we all make mistakes. That means no one can be perfect *and* authentic. But that doesn't stop us from trying.

As a recovering perfectionist, I've struggled with this for years. When I look back on my two decades on television, I'm amazed that I survived with my sanity intact. I'd set off a feeding frenzy when, heaven forbid, a hair got out of place. So I

No one can be perfect *and* authentic

shellacked my locks into place. My hair didn't move—it was teased, it was lacquered, it was a *helmet*. And yet, beneath the façade, I was still expected to come across as warm and authentic. My Q-score—a measure of popularity that can determine whether a television personality keeps the job or gets the boot—depended on it.

So what's real and what's not? And what does it matter, anyway?

Real versus Fake   Some leaders who were once branded "the real deal" were faking it in plain sight. Tour de France winner Lance Armstrong converted seven yellow jerseys into 87 million yellow wristbands—and hundreds of millions more in personal endorsement deals. But the former champion was disgraced and stripped of his titles and status when his use of performance-enhancing drugs was revealed in 2013.

Bernie Madoff was a former NASDAQ chairman turned financial advisor to high-society individuals and nonprofit organizations, an expert trusted by the elite to grow their financial assets. But in 2009, once his Ponzi scheme was exposed—along with the devastating reality that he'd inflicted up to $50 billion in losses on his clients—he was sent to prison.

And news of General David Petraeus's extramarital affair in 2012 undermined the reputation that he'd spent years building—among the Washington elite, with the thousands of soldiers he led, and with an adoring public.

The mismatch between what these people *wanted* us to believe and what we learned to be true made it clear that they weren't the real deal.

We are living in an almost excessively "faux" world. Think about it: you witnessed *faux singing* at Barack Obama's 2013 presidential inauguration. Pop singer Beyoncé later admitted that she lip-synched the national anthem because she wanted her performance to be perfect for the momentous occasion. And it *was* perfect—until the United States Marine Band threw her under the bus by exposing that she wasn't singing live.

You've seen a *faux girlfriend* exposed. The heart and soul of Notre Dame football's 2012 season, senior linebacker Manti Te'o, was humiliated when the touching story of his girlfriend's death—the narrative that catapulted him into the limelight and the Heisman Trophy race—was later exposed as an Internet hoax. Not only did this girl *not* die of cancer as Te'o had claimed, she *had never even existed*. Even worse, Te'o had told reporters that he was—*wait for it*—"completely devoted" to this girl—a fake person he'd never met. You may still be scratching your head over that one.

What's real and what's not?

As Catholic cardinals from around the world met ahead of the conclave to ultimately elect Pope Francis in 2013, a *faux cardinal* snuck in. An impostor wrapped a purple scarf around his waist and managed to slip past the Swiss Guard in Vatican City. The impostor shuffled right up to the real cardinals and even posed with Italian Cardinal Sergio Sebastiani before the guards noticed he was wearing a fedora instead of the traditional headgear. "He's not a cardinal—he's a fake!" they realized, and escorted him out.

It seems that no one and no place is sacred. What's real? And what's not? Shams and phony posturing extend beyond inner qualities to external features. Seemingly tight tushes are actually "Spanx'd" in place to conceal jiggling flesh. Glowing tans are airbrushed over pasty white skin. Voluminous-looking hair is clipped in to make thin tresses look fuller. The list goes on.

Tidy narratives trash the truth

Digital manipulation is especially rampant. Even network news anchors have been sucked into this vortex. When *CBS News* introduced Katie Couric as its new *CBS Evening News* anchor in 2006, the network admittedly Photoshopped her promotional picture to make her look 20 pounds thinner. Katie was fooled at first, too. "Wow! I look good," was her first impression, she told *More* magazine, before she learned of the electronic alteration.

Savvy television viewers realize their favorite so-called reality shows are anything but real. The performances are contrived and heavily edited—more trumped-up than Donald Trump himself.

Reality-show producers want to deliver tidy, audacious narratives that trash the truth. They want people to make spectacles of themselves to generate headlines. The programs have too much at stake to leave real storylines to chance. So they fabricate narratives, coach participants on what to say, and then cobble together provocative programs. Make it snappy. Chop, chop. If something is dull or lukewarm, they juice the footage by shuffling scenes out of order and out of context.

J. Ryan Stradal, a story editor on *The Bachelorette*, told *Time* magazine in 2006 that this technique is called "Frankenbiting." He explains, "We're using things said at different times, put together to imply a statement or observation." Of course, some producers beg to differ. They lean on author James Frey's "essential truth" defense. Tony DiSanto, executive producer of *Laguna Beach*, told ABC that the show was "enhanced" but genuine. Right.

Coming from a broadcast journalism background, I understand the editing-room mentality. Editing can transform run-of-the-mill interviews and facts into something much more compelling. It's akin to the ingredients in a salad—when everything's tossed together, the product comes out enhanced, depending on which ingredients you put in or leave out. My college professors trained me to keep it real; in the 1980s, the focus was on Journalism with a capital *J*. But today, with the Internet frontier providing an environment as wide open as the Wild, Wild West, that's certainly not the case anymore.

I also learned the protocol for how to present myself as a TV news anchor, a position that I held for many years. The first rule of anchordom is to project a spit-shined version of yourself. When you sit behind the anchor desk, act like a news anchor. Smooth out your rough edges.

Our opinions about and actions toward others flow from this one simple question: *Is this person the real deal?* When we believe that someone—particularly a leader—is the real deal, we trust them, we listen to them, and we willingly follow

We willingly follow the real deal

them. When someone doesn't strike us as the whole package, the opposite occurs. We suspect their motives and second-guess their ideas. We stall and sabotage instead of following their lead.

In the 13 years that I've been preparing to write this book, I've discovered why being the real deal is so crucial. I've explored the reasons as I studied leadership influence, working on the root causes of why some leaders have a consistently strong influence on their followers, while others manage to influence others only episodically.

I surveyed more than 3,500 leaders at my executive coaching sessions and corporate programs around the globe: the Americas, Asia-Pacific, Australia, and Europe. I interviewed leadership teams, sales teams, human resources professionals, engineers, and more.

Their answers electrified me and can change your approach to leadership.

What especially struck me was how people explained *why* they wanted to be influential. I kept hearing the words, "I want to be the *real deal*." At a recent corporate leadership class, I asked the seasoned leaders how they wanted others to view them. "One word," I said. Table by table, they revealed their one word aloud. Some shared terms like *powerful, influential,* or *bold*—but more than half answered *real. More than half.*

Being is more challenging than doing

They told me that *being* is much more challenging than *doing* and that most of leadership influence is achieved by learning how to *be*.

I believe the most powerful step you can take in the competitive modern marketplace is to be *real*. The sooner you develop this ability, the farther you will go. The benefits are clear. When you are the real deal:

You earn trust. People become committed to you and follow your lead; they respect and value your input.

You elevate performance. Not only your own performance, but that of everyone else around you.

You interface beautifully with the world. You're free from costly communication misfires and broken relationships.

The study participants went even deeper into why they wanted to be the real deal. They cited "presence" as a crucial factor—which raises the question, what exactly is *presence*?

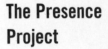

The Presence Project

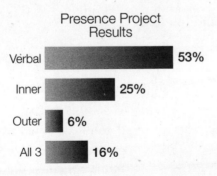

Presence Project
Results

Verbal	53%
Inner	25%
Outer	6%
All 3	16%

Of the 3,500 people surveyed, the largest group by far—53 percent—felt that their *verbal skills* give them presence and constitute the primary factor in their ability to influence others. The next largest percentage—25 percent—said their *inner presence* is most important to their leadership influence skills. A mere 6 percent believed that their *outer presence* made them influential.

Here's where it really got interesting: 16 percent attributed their influence to combining inner, outer, and verbal presence.

Let's focus on that 16 percent, since these are the ones who report they're able to consistently influence others. Who *are* these awesome people? How did they get there? And how do the rest of us get there, too?

The 3 Layers of Presence

When my team assimilated the answers, we discovered that the ability to be the real deal is based on what I now call *The Three Layers of Presence®*:

1. Inner presence

2. Verbal presence

3. Outer presence

Let's spend a moment discovering what these layers are.

....

Layer 1: Inner Presence
How You Experience Yourself

- If you're centered, you don't get caught up in your own head. You live your values and have a purpose greater than yourself.

- If you have *too little* inner presence, you're *The Worrier*. Anxiety may throw you off-center and cause you to lose influence.

- If you have *too much*, you're *The Egotist*. Narcissism may blind you and cause you to get stuck on your own needs.

....

- Verbal presence is the bridge between your inner and outer personas. If you're centered, your words Connect, Convey, and Convince®.

Layer 2: Verbal Presence
How You Reveal Your Messages

- If you say *too little*, you're *The Mouse*. Others miss the importance of what you're saying. They may ignore your communications.

- If you say *too much*, you're *The Motor Mouth*. You monopolize conversations. People are turned off and tune you out.

....

- If you're centered, people are drawn to you and trust you because they feel that you're authentic.

Layer 3: Outer Presence
How Others Experience You

- If you have *too little* outer presence, you're *The Ghost*— nearly invisible and easily overlooked.

- If you have *too much*, you're *The Pretender*. Something about you doesn't feel right to others.

....

Life has a way of knocking you off-center

These are the *Three Layers of Presence*—the proven path to influence and executive presence. Combine them, and you are consistently the real deal.

But here's the rub: each encounter, each person you interact with, forms its own unique situation. You may be the real deal with one person, totally centered in all three layers. But in other situations or with certain people, you're completely thrown off-center. Damaged relationships or bad habits may prevent your ability to show up as the real deal in those cases.

In this book, you'll read a lot about all three types of presence—and what may cause you to struggle to achieve them. You'll also discover how to handle someone else who's off-center. Think of presence as your center—like the center of a seesaw.

Life has a way of knocking you off-center, making you think you aren't enough.

Are you good enough?

I see this issue time and time again with my coaching clients. People fear they're not good enough, not smart enough, not attractive enough. So they puff themselves up to try to appear more impressive—or make themselves small and hope to fly under the radar. But we miss opportunities when we distort ourselves like this—whether we're adding a veneer or stripping a real layer away.

We may be reluctant to admit it, but many of us are motivated by the way the world perceives us. We enjoy recognition and status. It's not easy to free ourselves from the need for approval. But when we do, it changes the way we experience the world—and the way the world experiences us in return.

You have to develop and hone most business skills. But the most crucial skill is already inside you, ready to be let out. You don't have to be born with a set of special talents to become the real deal. You can discover your potential right now—which is something that you should find extremely encouraging!

Jim is a quiet but audacious man. He'd recently taken over as CEO of the world's number two organization in his field. He had a burning desire to make his organization take the leap to number one. As you can imagine, billions of dollars were at stake.

Jim's leap to become number one

"Is there one word that that sums you up?" I asked Jim at our first meeting. "Competitive," he responded, without even a second of hesitation. "I want to win. Always have. Ever since I was a snotty-nosed kid, I was never satisfied unless I won."

As we sat in his gleaming office, the afternoon sun dancing off a trophy case full of crystal awards, Jim explained his fervent wish to help his team become number one. "We're this close," he declared, with his forefingers just an inch apart.

Jim had hired a consulting firm to find out why his rival was winning over the marketplace. He wanted to learn why customers preferred them so his company could overtake them.

"Let me show you this word cloud from the consultant," Jim said. "This is the key."

A word cloud is a visual form of a weighted list. It's a twenty-first-century tool to make sense of a stream of data. When just a single word or two pop to the front of a word cloud, you've discovered gold. In this context, the consulting firm had uncovered how the marketplace perceived his rival—and how Jim could gain ground.

Word Cloud-Innovation

As you can see, the word "INNOVATIVE" popped out. Everything was congruent—the rival's clients, employees, even the company's marketing materials—describing the company with the term "innovative."

I asked Jim, "What did the research say about you? What's your company's word?"

Dead silence. He slumped back in his burgundy leather chair and looked at me with a pained expression on his face.

"We don't have one," he said. "People describe us in a lot of ways. But nothing pops out."

That's what stood between his company and his goal of becoming number one. The marketplace couldn't identify what made his company *the real deal.*

"What one word do you *want* people to use to describe your company, Jim?" I asked.

"Excellence," he said, without skipping a beat.

His team worked diligently for three years, rallying around excellence in everything they did. Internally, externally, in all of their communications.

Today, the competitive man's boldly stated goal has become reality. Jim's company is number one.

We can all take a lesson from this. Ask yourself, "What's *my* word? What word do I want to pop into people's heads when they think of me? What makes me the real deal?"

Imagine your word.

Better yet, don't just imagine it—write it down. Ponder it. Write down the word that you believe makes *you* the real deal. Don't worry if you aren't there yet. You can test different words and change your word throughout the course of the book. But ultimately, you should try to zero in on just one.

You'll return to this word cloud idea throughout the book. My goal is to help get you centered in all three layers of presence—centered *within*, centered in *how you communicate*, and centered in *how you come across to others* to be seen as the real deal.

As we go along, I'll share stories about people I've coached. My clients open up to me, and, as you might imagine, I sometimes have to tell them some

What makes you the real deal?

hard truths. I want you to learn from their experiences, but of course I will not betray their confidences. So I've changed their names and merged some of their situations together to protect their privacy.

The clients I'll tell you about have learned to stay centered. They've become the real deal. This book will help you answer the big question: are *you* the real deal?

I'll give you a hint now. The answer is yes.

You *are* the real deal. You always have been. This book will help you identify the situations and relationships that tend to tilt you off-center by giving you ways to center yourself.

Being real makes you worth following

Why is it important to develop all three layers when you could get by with one? Because to reach your full potential, you must engage your full self.

Beyond developing the talent and skills that your marketplace demands, your humanity is your most appealing virtue. Being real makes you trustworthy and worth following. Being real helps to improve everyone's performance, and it allows you to interface beautifully with the world.

You'll discover how to blend together all three layers of yourself to lead a balanced life. You'll find out how to integrate them into every aspect of your life and how to achieve the same steady presence in all situations.

You'll learn how to be the real deal consistently, not just episodically.

Your clients want you to be the real deal.

Your coworkers want you to be the real deal.

Most important, *you* want to be the real deal.

So let's get started!

LAYER ONE:
INNER PRESENCE

HOW YOU EXPERIENCE YOURSELF

Transform Yourself on Purpose

1

What Is Inner Presence?

Managing Yourself

Your inner presence can be your most valuable asset—or your deepest liability. I know that seems like a pretty bold statement—perhaps one you didn't see coming. Chances are, you're wondering what I mean by inner presence. So let's start with a simple definition:

Inner presence is the way you experience yourself.

That may sound a little spiritual, but it's actually a crucial *practical* skill. Inner presence determines the way you think, make decisions, lead, collaborate, and execute strategies. It directly influences your effectiveness.

Let's allow that notion to breathe for a moment. What's your first reaction? Is *your* inner presence an asset or a liability?

How you experience yourself

21

It's probably both. Why? Because, like so many things in life, the answer depends on the situation.

Your inner presence is a moving target. Your inner presence is a moving target from one moment to the next, since you experience yourself differently under different conditions. One day you beat projections for the quarter and your head swells with pride; another day, you lose a major client, and your confidence plummets.

Inner presence is what's happening inside your mind and heart as the world comes at you, judging you, testing you—even bringing opportunities your way.

Your inner presence is *a means to an end*. And a centered inner presence is vital if you want to take your performance and your leadership to the next level.

In my coaching practice, I've seen executives rise rapidly and crash spectacularly based on this single quality. *Everything* rides on it: Influence. Trust. Respect. Relationships. Reputation. Career.

I've discovered one thing, repeatedly and unmistakably: presence—what I call "the real deal"—*begins within*. It's about *being*, not just doing.

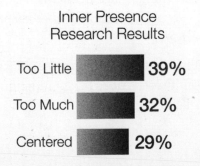

Inner Presence
Research Results

Too Little **39%**

Too Much **32%**

Centered **29%**

I've spent the past 13 years exploring how this works. I've surveyed thousands of leaders across industries and disciplines to find out how and why their presence affects their performance. When questioned about their views regarding the Three Layers of Presence, only 29 percent of respondents said they believed they were strongest in inner presence. The overwhelming majority felt their inner presence was unbalanced in one way or another.

Centering your inner presence is more important today than it's ever been. We live in a radically transparent society. Our organizations are flatter and more open than ever before. As leaders, we're always on—always in the spotlight. That means it's easier for our colleagues to catch us off-balance. And the pressure of our always-on world can itself throw us off balance.

Centering yourself will take work, but that work will pay off. When you're balanced, you set your talents free. When you learn to center your inner presence, you will live and work more effectively. You'll be freer. Happier. More powerful. More purposeful.

Freer. Happier. More powerful.

But when your inner presence is knocked off-center, you become a weaker version of yourself. Your capacity to lead and contribute suffers, as shown in the graphic.

Think of it as a seesaw. You want to be balanced in the middle. Too *little* inner presence and you're depleted, which can easily cause you to become anxious. Too *much* and you're full of yourself—and tend toward narcissistic behavior.

Steady or warped? Your current level of inner presence is a combination of where you came from and where you're trying to go. It's a sense of steadiness—or unsteadiness—drawn from your personal experiences. Most of us have an inner presence that's warped in one way or the other—which means we're wasting our potential. We're not making the impression we want to make, or influencing others the way we'd like. We don't lead the powerfully productive lives we'd like to live.

Remember the word cloud? It's a way to bring the big picture into focus by highlighting the most important themes.

In the Introduction, you chose a word that you would like to define yourself by—something that sums up the way you'd like to feel as you move through the world. Later, we'll talk about how you want other people to see you and hear your messages. But for now, this is all about you. Take another look at your word cloud in the previous chapter.

As you read the next three chapters, keep your word in mind. How often do you actually feel this way? What situations rob you of this ideal quality?

We all get thrown off-center from time to time. But if it happens too often, it will threaten your ability to advance in your career. It's up to you to shift the momentum. Ready to learn more?

2

Centered
Inner Presence

Steve's teams didn't know what to make of their new leader. He'd just acquired both of their businesses and consolidated them into one. Previously, a domineering bully had owned one unit, while a passive owner had run the other.

Transforming on purpose

"I've got two completely different cultures on my hands," Steve told me at our first meeting, as he described his site visits. "One group works heads-down. They've been conditioned to play it safe because their previous owner ripped them to shreds for years. The other team, who had an absentee owner, is like the Wild West. Everyone and everything is running amok; there's no accountability," he sighed, running a hand through his sandy hair.

Steve envisioned a new culture, similar to one he'd built earlier at another business. It was a culture where employees were transformed into leaders at all levels. He wanted everyone, regardless of their title, to be empowered and care deeply about their colleagues, customers, and suppliers.

"The hidden agendas are gone," he said. "I hope they can get past their skepticism, which I completely understand. They probably think everything I'm telling them is just lip service. They've never encountered leadership like this before."

Do you live your values?

Steve had strong values that balanced his solid work ethic. I'd never met anyone quite like him in a corner office. He was a wildly successful leader who truly focused on others, not on his own needs. When I asked him what he wanted to get out of working with me, he replied, "I'd like for you to help me develop a leadership team that's so remarkable that everyone in the entire organization feels energized and empowered. No phony baloney leaders who are all talk and no action. I want them to be the real deal."

Of course, he had robust financial goals, too. He wanted to double the company's book of business and profitability. This would be a stretch—especially since these once-separate companies had each disappointed their customers and underdeveloped their workforce in the past.

Steve believed that a culture focused on personal development would ultimately make leadership, staff, and customers happier and more effective. He wanted to invest in his people's development. He just needed to figure out how to make everyone else believe that he sincerely wanted them to reach their potential for themselves—and that he wasn't merely interested in his own profitability and success.

No leader wants his or her followers to see them as fake. Nobody wants their colleagues to suspect them of having a hidden agenda. We're all like Steve; we want the people around us to trust us. That foundation of trust and respect is the only way we can truly influence others.

Steve had already taken the first step toward his goal. He realized that in order to elevate his team's performance, he needed to be balanced internally. He needed to stay centered in order to get the best results for everyone.

He also had one other important advantage: his personal values. He valued respect, excellence, and humility and wanted to build a company founded on these qualities that would serve a purpose greater than profit.

"Values" and "purpose" may sound like fluffy distractions from the serious work of leading an organization in the twenty-first century, but they're not. They're actually the foundation for creating a *centered inner presence*—and that's the first step toward becoming the inspiring, compelling, effective leader you want to be.

What Centered Presence Looks Like

Did you watch the 2013 Super Bowl? If so, you might have caught the commercial called "So God Made a Farmer," showcasing a Dodge Ram pickup truck. It features the voice of the late, great radio commentator, Paul Harvey, delivering a snippet of his famous commentary. Though that speech is almost 40 years old, Dodge found Harvey's words inspirational. And so did Super Bowl viewers all over the world.

The speech made a strong impression because Paul Harvey was centered. He wasn't afraid to express his deep respect for others—in this case, farmers. Harvey was fully invested in the values he asserted. He wasn't hiding. He wasn't bragging. He praised the things he valued and criticized the things he didn't. He could give it to you straight, because he was straight on what he valued. Like him or not, he was the real deal. When he died in 2009, the ABC radio network could not replace him.

I recently interviewed Dr. Condoleezza Rice in front of a live audience that was gathered for a book signing of her autobiography, *Extraordinary, Ordinary People: A Memoir of Family*. The former secretary of state exceeded my high expectations because she was rooted in purpose: she wanted to honor her parents.

Yes, she gave a terrific interview, and the book-signing crowd loved her—but that's something most of us would have expected. She shared engaging stories about her parents, her experience accompanying diva Aretha Franklin on the piano, her love of football, and the most compelling people she met around the globe as the country's top diplomat.

But her purpose and her genuine warmth backstage before the interview were what truly caught me off guard. She was *centered*, and for some reason I hadn't expected that. It might have been because several book critics had taken shots at Dr. Rice's memoir, describing her writing as "aloof" and "distant." As a result, I expected a brusque, all-business presence to sweep into the green room, impatient to move on with the evening.

Instead, Dr. Rice was remarkably warm, thoughtful, and *razor* sharp. When I introduced myself, she even labeled us the "Connie and Condi" show. Despite her stature, influence, and accomplishments, she connected with every person in the room—individuals ranging from an intern to an NFL analyst. After the interview, the analyst remarked that Dr. Rice seemed to value gridiron wisdom and appeared to know as much, if not more, about the sport as he did. Talk about influencing a discerning audience!

Values and purpose combined are the foundation of your inner presence. Of course, you can't build a foundation on your values until you've defined what they are. This is your "big picture" approach to life, since you make choices based on what you value. You either consciously or unconsciously consult them when you decide whether to spend money, approve a project, take a job—and countless other things.

Are you invested in your values?

So, what are your values? Can you name them? Here's a list of some of the values clients have shared with me over the years:

What Do You Value?

achievement	growth
aesthetics	harmony
advancement	honor
authenticity	humility
boldness	integrity
bottom line	intellect
brevity	kindness
candor	loyalty
clarity	perfection
comfort	performance
compassion	philanthropy
competence	power
control	precision
cooperation	privacy
creativity	quality
decisiveness	recognition
discipline	reliability
education	reputation
efficiency	resourcefulness
empathy	respect
endurance	responsibility
enjoyment	safety
enthusiasm	security
equality	significance
excellence	simplicity
excitement	speed
expediency	stability
experience	status
fairness	teamwork
faith	thoughtfulness
family	tradition
flexibility	trustworthiness
freedom	uniqueness

I encourage clients to make a list of their top three values and establish a hierarchy. Which ones are most significant? Write down each value on the back of a business card. Stack them in order of importance from high to low. Then, use those values to help you make decisions going forward. If you're not sure what you value, think about where you spend your time, effort, and money. The place where these three intersect is where you'll find your true values.

Where do you spend your time, effort, and money?

Think about Yahoo! CEO Marissa Mayer's decision to bring her organization's remote workers back to the office. She stressed that she wanted Yahoo! teams to collaborate to move faster. Company data showed that *Yahoo!* employees working from home weren't accessing the company's remote network as often as they should have been—in other words, she felt they weren't productive enough. Mayer made the call to pull everyone back into the office to increase productivity and encourage collaboration. And she stuck by that plan despite the media hubbub that ensued. She valued productivity, teamwork, and expediency and she made her decision based on her values, not on what she thought employees or the public would prefer.

The bottom line is that if you want others to follow your lead, it's important to demonstrate and share your values so others aren't left guessing what they are. It will help to keep you and everyone around you centered.

So the next logical question is: what's your purpose? Having a purpose means being anchored by something greater than yourself. You

Your Purpose Is Your Power

must believe there's something bigger at play than you.

And by the way . . . there always is.

Try writing down your purpose with regards to your work. If you're stuck, imagine that you're receiving a lifetime achievement award. What would you want the announcer to say when she calls you up to the stage? Do you want to be recognized for making your industry more sustainable? For your dedication to meeting customer's needs? Maybe you'd like to be recognized for creating a corporate culture where all employees develop to their full potential. Think about the overarching goal of your work, and write it on the lines.

What's My Greater Purpose?

_____

_____

_____

_____

Figuring out your "purpose" might sound like quite a lofty goal—it requires some reflection. But discovering it actually makes everything else much easier. When you have a purpose, neither successes nor failures overwhelm you—because you're grounded. That's the end goal of being the *real deal*: to live a meaningful, purposeful life.

Traits of Centered Inner Presence

So what do Steve, Condoleezza Rice, Marissa Mayer, and other centered leaders have in common? What traits define a centered inner presence?

Merge Confidence and Self-Esteem

A centered person combines *confidence* and self-esteem, fights selfishness by *focusing on the external world*, and is grounded in a *reasonable view* of him- or herself. All three traits are related—but let's look more closely at each of them in turn.

Most people think that confidence and self-esteem are the same thing. I disagree. In my coaching practice, I've learned there are crucial differences between the two.

Confidence is the expectation of a positive outcome in a *specific situation*. It changes from day to day, which means you're in control. You can turn it on and off. Athletes do this all the time: They visualize themselves winning so that when they walk onto the field, they're confident. They believe they can win because they've visualized themselves doing it.

Self-esteem goes far deeper, cutting to your core. It's the underlying narrative you're created about your self-worth as a result of a lifetime of good and bad experiences.

You can be confident about today's big meeting even if you lack self-esteem, and you can have abundant self-esteem but lack confidence in your ability to deliver a great presentation.

Battle Selfishness

Lacking inner presence is *selfish*. I realize that sounds harsh, so let me explain. If you lack confidence or are too puffed up with pride, it means that you're focusing your attention squarely on *yourself*. And you actually have a choice: you can undermine situations by focusing on yourself, or you can redirect your focus to the external world and take yourself to a higher level.

If your inner presence is off-center, you prevent connections with others. Whether you've got *too little* inner presence and are worried about what other people will think, or you've got *too much* and you couldn't care less, you're at a disadvantage. You become so focused on how you're experiencing yourself that you can't see how others are experiencing your behavior. And while you don't realize it, you come across as self-absorbed. It may be a situational self-absorption—like temporary insanity—but that doesn't make it any less alienating to the people around you.

Narcissism and anxiety can look the same to the outside world; people simply feel that you're consumed with your own situation. They don't know your *intent*; they know only the *impact* you're having on them.

That's the key difference between a centered presence and an off-center presence. It takes internal reflection to get there, but the goal is to flip your focus to the external world. You want to be confident enough in yourself that you can put your energy towards working with the people around you—instead of staying trapped in your own head.

Measure Reasonably   Many of us get tripped up on the idea of perfection, and that warps our ability to see ourselves honestly. We focus narrowly on what we believe to be ideal, not on what's real. You'll read more about this later; for now, just know that it's important to develop a positive yet *reasonable* view of yourself. This will keep your confidence from rising and falling in response to every new situation and piece of feedback you encounter.

No one arrives in this world fully formed. You're a work in progress. Inner presence isn't a static goal that you achieve, and then you relax; it's a perpetual relationship with yourself.

Aim to strike a balance of confidence and humility. Be comfortable with the fact that you're not going to know all of the answers. Respect market leaders in your industry and know that there's a place for you, too. Resist the urge to compare yourself to others.

In their book *Egonomics*, authors David Marcum and Steven Smith point to four early warning signs that your ego is out of check:

Balance Confidence and Humility

1. Being defensive

2. Being comparative

3. Seeking acceptance

4. Showcasing brilliance

Genuine confidence doesn't exert itself. You don't feel like you have to prove yourself. You see both how far you've come, and how far short you are of what you're meant to be. If you strike the right balance, you'll have both long-term self-esteem and situational confidence. You'll find your equilibrium. You won't fall left or right of center—problems you'll read about in the following chapters.

If you're balanced, you can approach every new situation or challenge as an opportunity. You'll take your ego out of the equation, just like Dr. Rice did when—instead of demanding respect as the star attraction of the evening—she *earned* the respect of every person she encountered that evening, simply by being herself.

....

10 TIPS TO STAY CENTERED

Centered leaders draw on both self-esteem and confidence. Here are a few tips to help you become or stay centered:

1. **Define yourself.** Don't let *others* define you. That's the negative comparison trap. Instead, draw on your experiences—especially the bad ones—and use what you've learned. Own it. Create your own narrative.

2. **Don't shrink.** You're going to face intimidating people; we all do. Be aware that they will consciously try to overpower you when they smell fear on you. You can let yourself grovel—or you can firmly but politely hold your own. In the next chapter, you'll read about strategies to handle personalities like this. For now, know that you shouldn't shrink or wilt.

3. **Be a peer, not a peon.** Your goal is to be a trusted, strategic adviser, not an underling. You have the ability to do this within you. Be secure in the fact that you add value to

projects and people. You're a contributor, not merely a worker bee.

4. **Forget perfection: think excellence.** High performers often strive for flawlessness, which means aiming for the impossible. Think excellence, instead, to get over that self-limiting hurdle. Give yourself permission to be your best *at this moment*, not the best of all time.

5. **Expect a positive outcome.** Confidence requires you to tackle and wrestle your inner critic to the ground so you project a positive presence. It also means that your inner cheerleader will have to quiet down so you communicate more than a desire for self-preservation. Expect a positive outcome in a specific situation, motivate yourself to attain it, and you'll exude executive presence.

6. **Forget the peacock puffery.** Confident leaders don't puff themselves up at others' expense. They don't see colleagues as rivals to be outdone, or discard others' ideas as irrelevant. They don't disagree with others just because they didn't think of the idea. Humility is a treasured trait in leadership.

7. **Welcome feedback.** Fear of criticism is like *kryptonite* to a leader. It's a powerful deterrent that drains your confidence and power. Keep your humility in check by seeking feedback. That will help you transform your talents into bona fide assets and weaknesses into talents.

8. **Face it to fix it.** Fear of failure is a huge problem for leaders. If you can't face it, you

can't fix it. Tackle what you fear most as early as possible in your day. Don't avoid it. If you don't undertake it, it will inevitably pull you to your knees.

9. **Don't deal from disturbance.** Every challenge is an opportunity to center your inner presence. Don't deal with yourself from a place of disturbance; instead, choose to lean into a positive space. Your time here on earth is limited. Why spend it all shook up?

10. **Ask quality questions.** Be prepared before meeting with others. Know the material at hand so well that you help uncover the deeper "whys" beyond the basics. Probe for the true meaning and value. You'll build your competence along with your confidence.

....

A Centered Presence in Action

Unexpected challenges can knock anyone off-center. It happened to Steve: He wanted to focus his energy on improving his company's culture. However, the challenge of incorporating two new acquisitions in the midst of rapid growth destabilized him a bit. That's why he turned to a coach.

His goals were clear. He wanted to help every member of his company do work they could be proud of.

In one of our early meetings, Steve told me he wanted everyone to feel like they owned the company. It was a noble goal—but not one that I could envision working at the time. I explained to him: "Steve, *you're* the owner—*you* stand to reap the most financial rewards. You've also taken huge financial risks. How do you think your new teams would react if you asked them to 'think like an owner' without enjoying the financial benefits of being one? It's too soon after the acquisitions to make that kind of statement. They don't trust you yet. You'll face major push-back."

"You're right," he replied. "Let's come up with a Plan B."

Your journey begins with you

Steve worked thoughtfully to create an engaging workplace. He chose to invest in his team. He provided training and teamwork-building sessions. He was transparent in his decision making. He helped people develop their careers and move up in the organization. As a result, his company is soaring. But the journey began with Steve centering himself.

In the same way, your journey begins with you.

....

HOW TO INFLUENCE YOUR FELLOW SENIOR LEADERS

If you're a senior leader, your role is complex. You simultaneously manage your own business unit, function, or division while serving on a senior team that creates the organization's future. And maybe you're even vying with those peers for a higher spot in the succession plan. A balanced, engaging inner presence is the best way to influence your colleagues—and advance your own career. Here are a few tips on how to do that:

1. **Listen on purpose.** I've found that many leaders don't truly hear each other. They nix ideas before hearing others out because they slip into "Here's my two cents" mode. Listening is the desire to hear. The more vantage points you hear from smart people, the better. Better listening leads to better speaking and adds more value to your team.

2. **Choose cooperative over competitive.** Peter Drucker compared senior leadership teams to football squads because each member plays a fixed position. Therein lies the problem. Executive teams must overcome this inevitable fragmentation. You're competitive . . . and you should be. But look beyond the mission of your individual unit and ask yourself, "How can I cooperate with my colleagues in pursuit of a common goal?"

3. **Allow mutual, fluid influence.** You can't be an influencer unless you're willing to be influenced. Power-sharing is crucial when take-charge movers and shakers gather. Everyone craves respect—which means you need an extra dollop of self-awareness around other senior leaders. Stay open to mutual influence and adapt to the fluidity of the group.

4. **Help them help you.** Connect the dots for your fellow leaders. Guide them to see the big-picture issues of your unit. Don't assume that they know what's happening in your division.

Help reduce fuzzy vision by sharing compelling stories rather than ambiguous, text-laden presentations.

5. **Make it virtually possible.** Working together is even harder for global teams collaborating across multiple time zones. Contextual cues such as facial expressions and body language are not effective when we communicate cross-nationally. Reciprocal adaptation and respect for different styles are vital to developing trust and ensuring that critical viewpoints are heard.

....

3

Too Little
The Worrier

too little
"The Worrier"

Real
Deal

Values
and
Purpose

I first met Sharon on the 57th floor of her company's towering office building. She was whip-smart, driven, and thoroughly capable. She topped the succession plan as the heir apparent to the chief executive officer, who planned to retire the following year.

Whip-smart but anxious

Yet for some reason the CEO, Daniel, was starting to question whether Sharon could actually step into his shoes. He'd noticed a shift in her behavior over the past year, one that had been subtle at first but was now demonstrable. He was no longer certain that Sharon had the key characteristics and executive presence she'd need to lead the organization.

"She's become rushed and impatient," Daniel explained. "Her calibration is off." He felt that Sharon's ability to lead might be spiraling downward. So he brought me in to coach Sharon to regain her mojo.

When she sunk into the plush boardroom chair for our first meeting 10 minutes late, it was clear that Sharon was frazzled. "I'm under a microscope," she said with a sigh. "Everyone's a critic."

But no one was a harsher critic of Sharon than she was of herself. She was constantly judging her own performance. And she acknowledged that the heightened scrutiny—both internal and external—was hurling her off-center.

I asked her to identify specific situations that threw her off her game. "Let's start by identifying one," I said.

Do you feel scrutinized?

"Running late," she answered, noting that she'd arrived a few minutes late to our session. Sharon hated feeling like someone might be waiting on her. And unfortunately, someone almost always was waiting: on top of her high-pressure position leading a major business unit, she was raising two young children and tending an ailing parent. The constant pinging of her BlackBerry fed into the pressure, too. Sharon received e-mails at all hours of the day and night, and she disliked keeping anyone waiting on an answer.

Presenting to the board also heightened the pressure she experienced. "I'm a perfectionist," she told me, not surprisingly. As Sharon delivered presentations, she heard another conversation playing in her head. She was analyzing herself in real time, with her harsh inner critic acting as a color commentator, providing nonstop negative chatter.

"Sounds like 'snow-globe brain,'" I said.

"Yes, that's it!" she replied, relieved to be understood. "My brain is like a snow globe; all shook up with little particles floating around everywhere." She said that she had multiple ideas, thoughts, and running commentary competing in her head, all suspended in the air at once. She was *The Worrier*. And she couldn't find a path through the blizzard.

What Too Little Looks Like

U.S. Olympian Suzy Favor Hamilton focused on flawlessness. A middle-distance runner, she'd trained her entire life to win Olympic gold. And here she was, leading the pack in the 1,500-meter final at the Sydney Olympics in 2000.

She had only 200 meters to go. Just 30 seconds from winning the gold medal.

And then came the dive.

What happened? Suzy had fast legs, but an even faster brain. She felt the pressure of rivals on her heels and caved to it. As she explained to the *Milwaukee Journal Sentinel* in 2012, "There was nothing positive going through my brain. . . . Coming around that [last] corner, the anxiety gripped me so bad. It told my brain, 'Just fall. That's the easiest solution.

Just fall, and this all will go away.' That was the only way out."

The Olympian's internal presence was ruled by a negative inner voice—one that had convinced her that she was going to lose in the final seconds and suffer a humiliating failure. So instead of facing possible defeat, she feigned injury and took a dive to avoid the shame of losing.

Like many who battle the pressure of perfection, Suzy's body was intact—but her inner presence was off-center.

Ruled by a negative inner voice

In December 2012, Hamilton's life took another dive. *The Smoking Gun*—a website that posts legal documents, arrest records, and police mug shots on a daily basis—revealed that the three-time Olympian turned Wisconsin real-estate broker, wife, and mother of two, was secretly working as a call girl in Las Vegas. How do you free-fall from Olympic athlete to hooker? When pressed for a reason, Hamilton linked her double life to untreated anxiety, low self-esteem, and depression. *Suzy was The Worrier.*

Back to Sharon: she wasn't getting Olympic-level attention, but she was certainly feeling the pressure in the executive suite as her anxiety bubbled up. "How long have you been managing this?" I asked.

"My entire life," she said, noting that the pressure of the succession plan was aggravating her stress.

"Did you come from a critical family?" I asked.

"Bingo," she said, pushing her bob haircut behind her ear. "My dad was hypercritical." Her father, she explained, was also a driven high-performer. Throughout her life, he always seemed to find something negative to say—right through her years as a standout student and continuing with her steady ascent in the corporate world. Despite her many achievements, nothing was ever good enough for him—or, eventually, for her. He'd instilled a deep fear of criticism in her, and as a result, she secretly felt like an imposter. This apprehension about any form of disapproval and subsequent need to be perfect absorbed her so completely that she was afraid she'd be exposed as a fraud.

Have *you* ever felt that kind of fear? Can you honestly say that you constantly feel a centered inner presence? Or do you secretly worry, even occasionally, that someone's going to find out about your flaws? Do you obsess over your mistakes like Sharon? Do you hold yourself to a higher standard than you would ever hold a colleague, friend, or family member? Do you fear failing so badly that you might sabotage your success the way Suzy did? Would you rather fall than fail? Here are some of the common traits that define people with too little inner presence:

They're Often Perfectionists

Like Sharon and Suzy, perfectionists tend to get an extra dollop of positive reinforcement because they work so hard. They rack up praise, promotions, and awards. Consider the two examples from above: Sharon made it to the executive suite and Suzy made it to the Olympics. But perfection and anxiety can be, and frequently are, joined at the hip. Perfectionists often live with a constant fear that everything will fall apart if they let their guard down, and that others will blame them if anything goes wrong.

And people often misunderstand a perfectionist's intentions. Some may mistake their desire for flawlessness for a desire to have power over situations and people. Perfectionists are often labeled "control freaks" and defined as rigid, which overlooks the possibility their inner presence may be awry. People misread them because perfectionists are misaligned in inner presence.

If you're a perfectionist or work for one, you know all about their tendency to work extra hours and monopolize meetings in an effort to get things done "right." They do it because they're worried about living up to their own impossible standards. They're conditioned to believe that mistakes are intolerable, so they avoid errors at all costs—but their colleagues don't know that. So the perfectionist is misperceived as demanding and uptight.

Their language tends to be full of extremes and negative hyperbole. Words like "never," "terrible," "ever," and "always" are characteristic of the perfectionist.

The truth is that *everyone* makes mistakes. There are no exceptions. Missteps are a crucial part of the human experience. They help us to develop insights, gain empathy for others, and enhance our leadership capabilities.

The need to be perfect prevents you from seeing yourself clearly. Striving for flawlessness can make you overly critical of yourself and worried about how others will evaluate you. You set impossible goals, and then you beat yourself up for failing to reach them. Instead of judging yourself on a reasonable standard, you hold yourself up against an imaginary perfect self. You set yourself a test you're doomed to fail. And because you've failed, you can't focus on or appreciate the more realistic tests you're passing with flying colors. You may shrug off compliments, believing that you're not worthy.

They're Consumed by Criticism

Experts say that's where perfectionism often begins. Think about the way Sharon was analyzing her own performance while delivering a presentation. Instead of concentrating on and meeting the audience's needs, she was worried about how they were judging her ideas and appearance. Suzy, the Olympian, was so consumed by the notion of her possible humiliation that she failed to represent her country at the finish line.

You've just read about two women. However, I don't want to give the impression that only women exhibit this behavior. Plenty of my male clients are vulnerable to the same kind of threat to their inner presence.

Becoming more centered will ultimately help you escape perfectionism and other traps that reveal a deficit of inner presence. Keep reading and we'll get you there!

You may be thinking, "Am I just stressed out or am I anxious? And what's the difference, anyway?" After all, feeling uptight and apprehensive at times is part of life, right?

They Struggle with Anxiety

According to The Cleveland Clinic, stress is a normal, everyday feeling. Think of it as the normal background noise of a busy city block. Anxiety is *prolonged* stress, lasting six months or longer. It's the construction project next door that goes on for months, making the noise unbearable. Left unchecked, chronic stress can morph into generalized anxiety disorder, disrupting your life and leading to serious health concerns such as heart disease and memory loss.

Some people are more prone to anxiety than others. New research shows that anxiety may be hard-wired to some extent. A 2011 study in *Neuroscience and Biobehavioral Review*, the official journal of the International Behavioral Neuroscience Society, concluded that people who grow up in households rife with conflict may become hypersensitive to stress. They spend the rest of their lives hypervigilant, on edge, scanning for danger signs of conflict and criticism. For example, you may have learned to anticipate threats if members of your family vehemently argued a lot while you were growing up. According to the study, this can predispose you to respond more quickly and deeply when stressful situations arise.

Whether you're handling situational stress or chronic anxiety, your inner presence is more easily knocked off-kilter. You pay too much attention to yourself during these times—and not enough to the effect you're having on others.

I'm fascinated by how the pathways running through your brain regulate your thoughts and decision-making. Scientists are uncovering how the circuitry in your cerebral cortex—the brain's outer layer—often takes the quick and dirty shortcut to reach a conclusion . . . and why this sometimes sends you into a tailspin.

Dr. Margaret Wehrenberg is a Licensed Clinical Psychologist who studies where anxiety and irrational fears form—and shows people how to relieve them. In her book, *The Anxious Brain*, she points to the amygdala, a small clump of neural tissue on each side of the center of the brain. The amygdala is the seat of emotion and is capable of sending, you into high alert before you even process what's happening.

The anxious mind ruminates and avoids as the frontal cortex, including the amygdala, busily and desperately tries to avoid feeling the anxiety. Dr. Wehrenberg has coined a term for it: TMA—Too Much Activity.

Are you a "Productive Procrastinator"?

Her three-letter acronym nailed one of my vulnerabilities. When I'm stressed about a big project (like this book), I get cracking with a flurry of activity. I morph into a state that I call "The Productive Procrastinator." Everything gets done in a whirlwind of activity—everything, that is, except the project that triggered my procrastination. What am I worried about? Criticism. Rejection. Not being good enough. These are all issues that are probably rooted in things that happened to me a long time ago—but that's another story for another time.

How about *you*? Do you have a highly active mind? Do you ruminate and worry over possible scenarios in advance? Is it chronic? As I've seen in three decades of high-profile coaching and broadcasting, procrastination is one of the many ways the anxious brain wages war on itself.

Their Bodies Overrespond to Stress

Most people react to stress by tightening up physically. But those who are anxious take this reaction to an extreme in terms of muscle tension. You probably know people who fit into this category. Anxious people may suffer from temporomandibular joint (TMJ) disorder, neck pains, headaches, and a host of other health problems such as gastrointestinal issues and even bladder issues.

Relaxation does not come naturally to those with anxiety. When I rehearse with anxious high-profile leaders for their public appearances, I often see physical symptoms flood their bodies: their hearts race, their breathing turns rapid and shallow, and they have cotton mouth.

Sound familiar? Perhaps your face flushes, you sweat profusely, your hands tremble, your voice quivers, you have problems swallowing, or you feel shaky. None of these symptoms is fun on its own, of course; but bundle them together and you're a nervous wreck.

The symptoms and intensity of stress and anxiety vary dramatically from one person to the next. But one thing is constant—it's a cycle of a busy brain creating a tense body, which makes for an even more anxious brain, and so on.

The 2012 Oscar-nominated film *Silver Linings Playbook* features characters who are coping with chronic anxiety, among other mental health issues. The volatile, dysfunctional Solatino family is adjusting to life after their youngest son Pat is released from a psychiatric ward and moves back home with his parents. A former teacher, Pat flew into a violent rage when he found his wife, Nikki, in their shower with another man. It was prison time or the psychiatric ward. As part of a plea bargain, he chose eight months in a mental ward where he learned coping strategies.

In an early scene, we see Pat on his first out-patient visit to his psychiatrist's office. Stevie Wonder's classic tune "My Cherie Amour" is playing in the waiting room.

At that moment, Pat loses it.

First he barks at the receptionist to turn the song off and then, when she can't, he erupts in anger, overturning a bookcase.

Pat loses it

We soon learn that the song is a trigger that throws Pat's inner presence dangerously off-center—because it was Pat and Nikki's wedding song, and it was the song playing on the home stereo the day he discovered Nikki committing adultery. The tune now plays deafeningly in Pat's head, no stereo required, whenever he begins to feels off-center.

"Balance yourself," Pat's psychiatrist urges him. "Recognize the feeling that comes to you. Work on a strategy."

Though strategizing is not Pat's strong suit, he does develop a plan. He becomes a compulsive jogger to minimize his anxiety, while wearing a black plastic garbage bag to maximize weight loss.

The movie is both profound and funny as Pat struggles to stay centered.

We're all damaged souls

Pat is a lost soul. The truth is that we're all damaged souls in one way or another. Everybody gets off-center (though hopefully not enough to warrant doing time or facing a restraining order). Like Pat, we all have triggers that set us off—and most of us could use a playbook when anxiety strikes.

Tips to Increase Inner Presence

Here is a set of guidelines you can use to build your strategy:

Identify your triggers. The first step is to pinpoint what consistently knocks you off-center. Like Pat, you need a strategy when you're provoked. What kinds of situations make you tense up and feel anxious? Ambiguity feeds anxiety. Therefore, identifying situations and conditions that cause you to spiral out of control can help you create a plan that will keep damaging, destructive behaviors at bay. You can usually home in on these by taking stock of your physical condition or reactions as well (more on that later).

Silence your inner critic. Shut down the annoying roommate in your head—the one who's dishing out harsh commentary about your performance. Don't stress yourself out by anticipating criticism that may never come. Recognize the chatter inside your head as a "thing" instead of an emotion. It's neurotic. Let it go. Push it away. You may want to come up with an affirmation or mantra you can use as a response to anxious thoughts when they arise.

Manage your shock clock. Build in margins between important activities to give your nervous system a break. Don't be a slave to an overstuffed calendar. Regroup at least once a day to process ideas—especially after idea-rich meetings. Manage your clock to refocus on the big picture: otherwise, your day will get away from you.

Control your cortisol surge. You've doubtless heard of adrenalin and the effects it has on your body. But did you know that your brain releases a surge of the stress hormone cortisol when you're anxious? A flood of cortisol can impair cognitive performance and spike your blood pressure. How can you counter it? Take note of *specifically where* your body radiates physical tension. Is it your shoulders? Your jaw? Your hands? Consciously calm those muscles and you'll help overcome the cortisol.

Reject negative notions. If you get stuck on a negative thought, ruminating on it and obsessing over it can trigger a tailspin. Quietly but firmly tell yourself "no" or "stop" when you're stuck on a negative thought. If you notice what you pay attention to and envision positive instead of negative outcomes, you can gain the upper hand.

Get moving. Studies show that exercise helps prevent stress and anxiety. It also eases the symptoms when you feel it coming on. According to the Cleveland Clinic, keeping fit releases feel-good brain chemicals such as endorphins. If you're overstressed, you may feel like you don't have enough time to take care of yourself—but that's the precise time when you need it most. If you skip self-care, you make your anxiety worse.

Pump more oxygen. Breathing deeply from your diaphragm activates a calming signal that frees your mind. Most of us slip into shallow respiration when we're stressed, drawing air only from our larynx, where speech is produced. This is more damaging than you might think. Your brain, sensing oxygen deprivation, slips into fight-or-flight mode. If you can learn to breathe deeply from your diaphragm, it will help free your brain.

Journal it. The next time you feel anxious, try to write about what's happening to you in as much detail as possible. What does it feel like? What happened that might have set you off? Are there actions you can take that would make you feel calmer? See if you can track your symptoms back to their source. Another option is to keep a gratitude journal. Before bed, write down three things you were grateful for that day. This will help calm your brain before sleep.

Cut the caffeine. Caffeine has a profound effect on the nervous system, and can contribute a great deal to anxiety. Research has shown that caffeine consumption tends to overstimulate the brains of anxious-prone individuals. Worriers are more likely to trigger performance-debilitating anxiety if they stimulate their nervous systems with caffeine. Don't worry, you can cut back gradually! When you crave a jolt of energy, do a few jumping jacks or take a walk around the office to perk yourself up. Or substitute an herbal tea for your afternoon coffee, so you can keep your ritual without overcaffeinating yourself.

Give yourself a stimulation break. Caffeine isn't the only stimulant. Many people in our always-on, über-stimulated society feel they need to provide instantaneous responses to every voicemail, e-mail, or tweet. Your phone beeps, chirps, and sings, your computer sucks you in like a magnet—and every time something pings, your brain receives an alert. You may find that you can't calm it down until you respond to the demand. Set aside time in your schedule when you can turn off the incoming alerts and get some real work done.

Don't expect a perfect choice. An anxious brain believes there's a perfect choice. There's not. If you aren't satisfied with anything but perfection, you'll never be satisfied. You'll be trapped in a vicious cycle of finding—or creating—problems, solving them, and then finding more.

Deliberately worry well. There will be some legitimate concerns you must address. You should focus on them—but set a time limit. Ten minutes should be enough. And don't use this time to dream up worst-case scenarios but instead to make a plan to solve the problem that's worrying you. Make a list, prioritize it, and set time limits for each step. Ambiguity feeds anxiety. Make a list of your concerns and get down in black and white and you'll worry *productively*.

No matter what triggers your stress or anxiety, I urge you to take action to center your inner presence if you want to be the real deal. You'll feel more powerful, build better relationships, and get better results—not only from yourself, but from everyone around you.

How to Manage *The Worrier*

What if the anxious brain isn't *yours*? Perhaps you live or work with (or *for*) a worrier. If so, you know they can shift from relaxed and productive to frenzied and fractured in a heartbeat. They can suddenly get caught up in a whirlwind in which everything seems urgent.

TIPS

Here are some tips to help them cope:

Turn down the wattage. What person living in our fast-paced world *isn't* susceptible to Sharon's "snow-globe brain" problem, at least on occasion? When you notice that someone has slipped into overdrive and is all shook up, turn down the volume. Eliminate extraneous noise and distractions and help them concentrate.

Take on one issue at a time. Don't overload a Worrier; prioritize. Worriers are drawn to checklists, so encourage them to list items in order of descending importance, and to tackle the biggest projects first. Checking off important tasks can help them regain their balance. I told Sharon's boss she needed clearer priorities, and they worked together to triage her most important tasks.

Single-tasking is the new multitasking. Performing two or more tasks simultaneously or switching back and forth between tasks can cause mental blocks. Studies show it reduces productivity and spikes stress. If someone is stressed, help them refocus and work *on one thing at a time.*

Guide them to be more resourceful. Worriers are naturally problem-centric, not solution-centric. So find a way to model resourcefulness for them. If they're stuck, encourage them to use all of the resources at their fingertips. Google searches, YouTube video demonstrations—the digital world is loaded with ways to get unstuck if they simply switch to a resourceful attitude.

Recognize them spontaneously. Respect and appreciation are basic human needs that serve as a powerful antidote for stress. Sincerely recognizing someone's efforts is powerfully reinforcing for them—even more so when it's unexpected. Plus, the benefit to this approach is that people repeat what they're rewarded for. I gave this hint to Sharon's boss, too—positive reinforcement supported her as she worked to let go of her fear of criticism.

Operation Slow Down, Sharon

Remember Sharon's snow-globe brain? She was stuck in a cycle where her fear of letting anyone down caused her to rush, and then the rushed feeling fed into impatience, and so on. We began our work together with something I dubbed "Operation Slow Down, Sharon."

We attacked the problem both internally and externally, using many of the strategies from the action plan above. First, Sharon faced her anxiety and identified it for the first time. Then, we reshaped her schedule to keep it at bay. For example, instead of checking e-mail first thing in the morning, Sharon now starts each day focused on her big-picture priorities while she's fresh. We also built in margins to her calendar. She schedules downtime between meetings and other events whenever possible so that she won't have to run from one thing to the next. And we added a weekly lunch with important colleagues to her calendar. This is helping her cement relationships and combat feelings of isolation.

We also made some physical changes. Sharon recognized that she slips into shallow respiration when she's stressed, which she's combating by taking deeper, slower breaths. And she's taken up yoga—something that sounded tedious to Sharon until she realized that's precisely *why* she needed it—to slow down her racing mind. She's also exercising more.

Did "Operation Slow Down, Sharon" work? It did. Daniel was delighted with Sharon's transformation and she assumed the role of CEO when he retired. She's now centered in her inner presence while thriving in the corner office.

It can work for you, too.

....

THREE STEPS TO BREAK THE PATTERN OF PERFECTION

Are you falling into the perfection trap? Is this your Achilles' heel? The following three quick tips will help you center yourself.

1. **Name It.** Most perfectionists don't think of or label themselves as perfectionists. They consider themselves *detail-oriented*, and don't realize how much their habits disrupt their inner

presence. Repeat after me: "I'm a perfectionist, and it's time to stop."

2. **Listen for Extremes.** If you catch yourself using one of those telltale perfectionist terms like "always," "never," "terrible," or "ruined," stop and rephrase your sentence—and you'll change your mind-set as well. Give yourself credit for catching yourself in the act.

3. **Plan for Imperfection.** Once you've identified the problem and caught yourself in the act, start planning for imperfection. It'll be easier to tolerate the inevitable flaws when you recognize that perfection isn't the goal. Making a contribution is. Moving forward is. Leading is. Think of the 80-20 rule, which states that roughly 80 percent of the outcomes can be attributed to 20 percent of the efforts. The 80–20 rule is a beautiful thing—accepting 20 percent imperfection can help you conquer your inner beast!

4

Too Much
The Egotist

too much
**"The
Egotist"**

It was becoming clear that either James or David would have to go. The friction between the two leaders was tearing their company apart. Separately, the Senior Vice President of Sales and the SVP of Brand Marketing served their business units well. They had immense cachet as members of a highly visible, powerful team. But they could barely stand to be in the same room together, which made executive team meetings fragmented, frustrating, and highly stressful. Decision making was laborious and sometimes impossible.

They couldn't stand each other

Their CEO asked me to help solve this senior leader crisis. "One of them has to *give* or one of them has to *go*," Paul said, his cheeks turning red. I could almost see the smoke billowing out of his quickly graying head of hair.

James didn't see the problem. As the head of the company's sales unit, his metric was the numbers, and they were rising steadily. "Who cares if I take a few digs at David?" the tall, burly man said with a grin in our first meeting. "He's too uptight. I'm just busting his chops." James couldn't understand why the CEO was making such a fuss about interpersonal issues and so-called dysfunctional dynamics.

David, on the other hand, was contemplating leaving the company over the conflict. He found James's behavior intolerable. David, a star performer all his life, said that James's sarcastic comments and zingers demeaned and belittled others in senior leadership meetings. "He's an egomaniac, a blowhard," he told me. "He tosses blame like hand grenades. He even talks about himself in the third person. What a narcissist!" he sighed.

Colleagues saw him as a bully

David wasn't the only one affected by James's domineering personality. The sales team was feeling it, too, and some of them had had enough. The turnover rate had recently picked up. But even as his staff abandoned ship, James could save any account with a personal visit to the customer. He was a charmer: clients loved his sense of humor and colorful stories, and thought of him as a fun guy. But his colleagues saw a different side of him.

James didn't seem to appreciate the fact that his job was at stake. Paul was ready to cut him loose if the team dynamics didn't improve.

The situation had arrived at a pivotal turning point. I knew I had to get directly to the heart of the matter to redefine the problem and transfer ownership of the issue to James. I started simply. "What do you think is your single most important quality?" I asked.

Initially puffed up, he suddenly turned reflective. That's when he said something very interesting: "I see myself as the alpha wolf in a pack of hunters." There it was—*the alpha wolf*. He saw himself as the head of the hierarchy. The top of the social structure. The first to eat after the hunt.

His colleagues saw him as a blowhard bully, but James saw himself as a leader's leader. How did this happen? Could he fix it before being fired? Or would David walk out first?

What Too Much Looks Like

"You feel invincible," John Edwards said of his days as a presidential contender. "Running for president fed a self-focus—an egotism, a narcissism that leads you to believe you can do whatever you want."

There it is again: the "n" word—*narcissism*—torpedoing another career.

In a 2008 interview on ABC's *Nightline*, the philandering Edwards labeled himself a narcissist and admitted that his time in the spotlight had gone to his head.

"Edwards used terminology that others had not dared to use," said Wendy Behary, author of

Disarming the Narcissist and founder of the Cognitive Therapy Center of New Jersey. Edwards was an innovative narcissist, apparently ahead of his time by self-identifying his ailment. Nowadays, we toss the term around like a football on Thanksgiving.

You may have heard it again following the fire hydrant crash heard 'round the world. Tiger Woods admitted to being a self-absorbed narcissist in his televised mea culpa, following his 2009 cheating scandal. "I never thought about who I was hurting. "I thought only about myself." I thought I could get away with whatever I wanted to," said Tiger, who sought counseling to "become a better man."

"I thought only about myself"

Lance Armstrong confessed to both doping and narcissistic behavior in a steady drumbeat of riveting yes and no questions during his January 2013 interview with Oprah Winfrey on her television network, OWN. The disgraced champion acknowledged launching damaging rumors and personal attacks against anyone who dared to challenge his deceit over the years. He still appeared defiant in the interview—admitting the truth but unwilling to confront the reality of his behavior.

So let's back up for a minute. Do you recognize any of this behavior? Maybe you haven't put a label on it, but some of these stories sound familiar.

Identifying an Egotist

What's the difference between a garden-variety self-centered blowhard and a narcissist?

Psychologists say you can often identify a narcissist by these behaviors:

- A grandiose sense of self-importance
- Self-absorption
- A sense of entitlement
- Impulsiveness
- A craving for admiration
- A preoccupation with power
- A lack of empathy
- A judgmental, critical attitude
- A belief that the rules don't apply to them
- Intolerance to setbacks or perceived slights
- Explosive anger when frustrated

If John Edwards, Tiger Woods, and Lance Armstrong represent a common endpoint for narcissistic behavior, where does the journey start?

Essentially, *The Egotist* starts in the same place *The Worrier* does. But where the anxious personality gets stuck in that self-doubt, the narcissistic personality pushes it away, craving and focusing on the praise that proves those doubts wrong.

They Feed their Ego

"There is a euphoria attached to the relentless feeding of the ego," says psychotherapist Dr. Samuel Lopez De Victoria, known affectionately as Dr. Sam. "The grandiosity in their own mind tends to make them so vain that an illusion of

They're Addicted to admiration

invincibility is created," he said in an August 2008 interview with ABC News.

Their behavior may begin with fawning fans or flattering parents. Whatever the origin, Dr. Sam says, "They are insensitive to the reality of events and relationships around them until they fall off the skyscraper and find that the law of gravity applies to them, too."

Turns out, the narcissists' biggest battle is figuring out how to center themselves. They can become so intoxicated by their own power that it knocks their inner presence off-center. Puffed up by praise and addicted to admiration, they get high on their own hype.

They want others to see them as all-powerful, but the hidden truth is that narcissists often have low self-esteem. They're easily bruised by criticism. Perhaps that explains why some of your self-centered colleagues howl at the moon in retaliation when they think you've done them wrong. They don't just get even, they get revenge.

I'm astounded by how often corporate clients and keynote audiences pull me aside to define their colleagues as narcissistic. Here a narcissist, there a narcissist, everywhere a narcissist! Most people seem relieved to learn that they're not the only ones on the receiving end of the hissy fits.

They Demand Praise

In the workplace, narcissists often enter a room as if to a blare of trumpets. Have you noticed how their power walls are adorned with plaques and pictures? Or how they surround themselves with deferential people whose attitudes toward them are a mixture of worship and contempt?

The praise they demand from the people around them hints at the true cost of narcissism in the workplace. A narcissist and an anxiety-ridden person are a toxic human cocktail. The anxious person throws himself into a tizzy trying to please the unpleasable, while the narcissist makes demands, lobs verbal grenades, and wreaks havoc. Like it did with James and David, workplace tension and dissatisfaction can skyrocket when the two collide.

They Hide a Dark Side

A self-absorbed person is often a tale of two faces. If you work with or are related to one, you know that dealing with them can be downright unpleasant. And yet people outside the office or the family find them charming. Internally, their words are harsh and biting. But externally, they can dial it back a notch and be witty.

They can also bully or bluff their way through any crisis. As I saw in my 20 years in broadcast television studios, egomaniacs go on power benders when others challenge them. My position at the anchor desk gave me a front row seat to plenty of people who expected that everyone would trust their words more than the facts. I watched in amazement as they tried to talk their way out of dire situations. You've likely seen the same thing in your business. Maybe you've watched a power-monger put half-baked ideas on the table or subpar products on the market. Their judgment is impaired because they're focused only on their own feelings.

So why do they get away with it? Some of the personality traits that come with narcissism can be productive, like a natural desire to lead. Leaders often put up with their excesses because they produce results—until their attitude starts to harm the culture enough that something has to be done. That's what happened to James, of course. His attitude became toxic enough that Paul was braced to give him the heave-ho.

Toxic enough to get the "heave-ho"

It happened to another salesperson at a Fortune 500 firm whose leadership team I coached. Debbie was the highest performer on her sales team. Customers loved her, but her coworkers couldn't stand her. She refused to turn in her expense reports because she thought it was menial work. She'd get furious if she was asked to come to a meeting—apparently meetings were beneath her, too. And she flew into a rage when they switched her sales territory, ranting endlessly to anyone in earshot about how unfair the change had been.

Debbie's CEO, Linda, wondered if her star salesperson was coachable. As Linda and I were standing in the hallway, Debbie approached. Apparently, she was ready for her coffee. She spotted her department's assistant coming down the hall, balancing an open laptop in one hand and an armful of small equipment in the other. Debbie turned to us and said, "Here comes my mule now."

My *mule*. That was the core of Debbie's problem. She didn't care one bit that the assistant was overburdened and obviously on her way to a conference room. All she cared about was getting her coffee—stat.

Anxiety and narcissism may stem from similar places; but while an anxious person's obsessive worry about what other people think makes them *seem* caught up in themselves, a narcissist who gets too far off-center *actually will* stop being concerned about other people's feelings.

They Ignore People

Of course, Debbie should have cared about what her colleagues thought. And if she'd known how *self*-destructive her behavior was, she might also have been concerned about the toll her attitude would eventually take.

A study by researchers at the Universities of Virginia and Michigan found that people with narcissistic qualities might be at higher risk for certain health problems. The study focused on men and showed they had higher levels of cortisol—the same stress hormone that floods the anxious brain. Of course, the narcissistic personality is more likely to jump into fight mode than flight mode, but the stress is still just as real, and just as damaging. The research showed that people with narcissistic qualities are at greater risk of high blood pressure, heart problems, and other stress-related illnesses.

Addicted to Social Media Followers

How many Facebook friends do you have? This may sound like a frivolous question, but it's related to the topic at hand. Researchers at the University of North Carolina Wilmington and the University of Hartford found via a recent study of college students that those with extremely high numbers of Facebook friends are more likely to have narcissistic qualities. According to another study done at Western Illinois University, spending more than an hour a day on the site—or tagging yourself in tons of photos—can also be warning signs. And that goes for other social networks, too: frequent tweeting about yourself is associated with narcissistic traits.

Age may play a role here, too. Younger generations show more narcissistic tendencies than their forebears. An analysis of the annual CIRP Freshman Survey by psychologist Jean Twenge, author of *The Narcissism Epidemic*, found that narcissism among students is increasing—even as basic skills are decreasing. A growing number of young people describe themselves as "above average." But this isn't Lake Woebegone; all the kids can't be above average. Honest self-evaluation is an important skill in any field. As former Indiana University basketball coach Bobby Knight says in his book *The Power of Negative Thinking*, it's a virtue to know your weaknesses and work hard to counteract them.

Most important, it's essential to have a realistic view of your relationships with your colleagues. Are you like James—receiving praise from clients, but feuding with those closest to you? James didn't even bother to start e-mails with a greeting; he jumped straight to telling the other person what he needed. That attitude may work for a while, but it will eventually alienate the people around you. And it will hold you back if you want to advance.

Even before his public and private life fell to pieces, fellow golfers said that playing around with Tiger Woods was an intimidating experience. Woods wouldn't talk to them, instead delivering what came to be known as the "Tiger treatment." Masters champion (2003) Mike Weir told *Sports Illustrated*, "It isn't something you can prepare for, it's something you have to experience, and even then there's no guarantee you can handle it."

How to Dial Back Too Much Inner Presence

Woods certainly didn't rush to make amends for his bad behavior. He took his time apologizing to fans after the scandal broke. But when he finally stepped up to face the media 80 days later, it appeared that therapy or a good PR team, or perhaps both, had helped him gain perspective on his self-centered behavior. While his delivery was stiff, the content of his apology was strong. Here's why:

1. **He didn't sidestep.** He focused on the hot-button issues: he cheated, he alone was to blame, he was sorry for what he'd done, and he was taking steps to ensure that it would never happen again.

2. **He focused on the people he'd hurt.** He acknowledged that people had good reason to be critical of him. His target audiences for the apology were his soon-to-be-ex-wife and immediate family, his business partners, and his fans. He was specific about how he'd let each of them down.

3. **He stated the solution.** He shared exactly what he was doing to try to make things

right—going to therapy and working on his issues. He also pointed out that he was returning to his faith after drifting away. He said that he was working to ensure that he never repeats the mistakes he had made.

If Tiger can conquer his narcissism, it will be the story of redemption beyond the golf course that will offer hope to everyone out there who's gotten a little too caught up in themselves.

Hopefully *you* haven't done anything destructive enough to warrant a televised apology. But if you've been alienating your colleagues with self-absorbed behavior, you will need to help them feel that they can trust you again.

Help others trust you

Let's return to James. The first and most important step he had to take was to clear the air with David. And that's exactly what he did. He approached David, extended his hand, and said, "I'm sorry that things have gotten out of control. I didn't realize how much I was at fault. Can we start over?" Like Tiger, James didn't sidestep the problem. He learned to be straightforward about the issue, admit responsibility for his part in it, and sincerely state his willingness to be part of solving it.

Of course, there are times when a single apology won't be enough. Lance Armstrong's short-lived *Tour de Apology* was proof of that. His larger-than-life behavior had popped like an overinflated balloon, but many people didn't sense any real change in his behavior. And while you're probably not operating at that scale, you may also need to change your behavior in order to win back the trust of the people around you.

If you're beginning to notice that your own self-centered behavior skews toward The Egotist, *here are some strategies that will help you rebuild your relationships and get centered again:*

Make time to connect. Narcissists tend to ignore the people around them and instead focus on how they can get the admiration they crave. James realized he sometimes got into what we called his "beaver behavior": he just wanted to build that dam, so he'd look past the people around him and do, do, do. If this is you, consider doing what James did by deliberately building in-person conversations into your schedule.

Start conversations with a positive comment. People will find it abrupt and hurtful if the first thing you say when you walk into a room is negative or critical. Keep other people's feelings in mind. You don't have to sugarcoat all your comments or say anything you don't mean; but do try to imagine how *you'd* want to hear feedback. James felt awkward the first few times he tried this, but as he got used to it, he realized starting on a positive note did change the tone of his conversations.

Fight EUI and TUI (e-mailing or texting under the influence). If provoked, don't fire off an angry response immediately. Wait until you cool down and you can think more carefully about how the recipient will react to your e-mail. And while you're waiting, reflect on what's triggering your anger. Do you tend to overreact to criticism or to colleagues' encroaching on your turf? Can you try to see the situation from the other person's perspective?

Seek commitment, not compliance. Don't just bark orders. Help people understand *why* something needs to be done, and they'll be more likely to support you. James had to learn to speak to David about his ideas before board meetings. David automatically opposed James's ideas when he felt blindsided. But a little advance notice made him feel like a partner. You can't bulldoze people into doing what you say if you want them to genuinely care about and commit to it.

Transfer ownership. Don't hog the limelight. You may crave attention because you have low self-esteem. But the more sustainable way to build a good reputation is to make sure your colleagues see you as a collaborator, someone who contributes without controlling. The next time you're praised for a project, acknowledge a colleague's contributions. If you're the leader, fight the urge to micromanage. Let your employees take true ownership of their assignments.

How to Manage an Egotist

Maybe you're not the Tiger who needs to be tamed. If you're working with someone who matches the descriptions you've just read, don't despair. Here are a few tips—some from my book on interpersonal skills *Talk Less, Say More*—to make life bearable while you deal with narcissist in your life:

Don't "cope with" the behavior—manage it. Coping and managing are two fundamentally different mind-sets. Coping makes you a victim, while managing puts you in control. So switch your mind-set. Don't let The Egotist knock you off-center.

Give them options. Beneath their bluster, narcissistic people fear being left out of the loop. They crave control. It's far better to offer them options to choose from than to feed them other people's ready-made decisions, which they'll want to tear into shreds. Giving them choices helps them feel respected and in control, and prevents nasty hissy fits.

Focus on solutions, not problems. When you explain a problem or a challenge to an Egotist, direct their attention to the solution. Don't let them dissect the problem over and over again. Narcissists love drama and revel in chaos. They're also easily agitated when frustrated. Define problems clearly and present possible solutions right away, so they don't smell blood in the water and tear you apart.

Let them think it's their idea. Narcissists often steal the credit for ideas that aren't theirs. Why do they do that? They want attention badly enough that they actually rewrite history in their minds. However, if this gets things done, I say learn to live with it rather than protest. Everyone will catch on over time. Meantime, graciously transferring credit for ideas to the narcissist makes things happen.

Manage their emotional blind spot. Egotists lack empathy. They're so caught up in their own world that it doesn't occur to them to consider your feelings or viewpoint. It's a huge blind spot.

So if you want them to know how you feel, you're going to have to tell them. Just be smart about it; some narcissists will pounce on what they see as weakness with criticism or guilt trips.

The Egotist needs to focus on others

The bottom line is, just like *The Worrier, The Egotist* needs to shift focus from themselves to others. If you think you might have too much inner presence, ask yourself, "Am I wrapped up in myself and my own reputation?" If the honest answer is yes, try to remember that you'll build a better reputation and inspire more meaningful work from the people around you if you focus on *them*.

This approach worked for James. After he changed his attitude toward David and his other colleagues, his sales team stepped up to the plate and started landing bigger and bigger accounts. He transformed into an inspiring leader. Building better relationships with his colleagues improved his department's culture, and that led to skyrocketing sales. Last but not least, it saved him his job! Today, he's the president of his company.

If James can re-center himself, so can you.

....

HOW TO APOLOGIZE EFFECTIVELY

If your inner presence is off-center, chances are you have some apologies to make. Some people rush to retract big transgressions merely to protect their backsides, which people perceive as insincere.

Others overapologize for small acts, dripping with contrition, which damages their credibility. Both of these tactics are ineffective. Like antibiotics, apologies lose strength when they're misused.

The trick is to understand *the art of the apology* and follow the right steps. Here are some tips culled from my first book, *Talk Less, Say More*, to generate goodwill with a contrite but classy apology:

1. **Hit the hot button.** Focus specifically on the emotional hot button. If you're criticized for being irresponsible, for example, apologize for your lack of judgment.

2. **State the solution.** If you've created a problem, say exactly how you're going to make it right. This will protect you from future criticism.

3. **Focus on the recipient.** An apology involves much more than a quick "Oops—sorry!" Make sure the recipient knows that you fully understand the impact of your transgression and that you won't let it happen again.

4. **Don't blame the victim.** You'll sound pompous and insincere. Don't begin with "If I offended anybody . . ." That sounds like you're blaming a resentful person for being overly sensitive to remarks that you feel you obviously didn't intend as an affront. Instead, take responsibility. Say something like, "I offended you and I'm sorry."

5. **Time is of the essence.** Apologize as soon as possible. In today's Internet age, you can't wait

for the web to spread bad news before you express your contrition, or people will be convinced that you're guilty and don't care.

6. **Don't inflict more wounds.** Phrases such as "No offense, but . . ." and "Don't take this personally, but . . ." are passive-aggressive. You're saying one thing, but you mean the opposite. What you're about to say *is* personal and yes, it's likely to offend. So instead of qualifying it, be honest and get to the point kindly but decisively.

Let's face it—we're all human. Which means that we're all prone to messing up and hurting someone else's feelings from time to time, even when we don't intend to. The key to apologizing effectively is to handle it directly, sincerely, and as swiftly as possible.

···

TOP 10 TIPS FOR CENTERING YOUR INNER PRESENCE

1. **Silence your inner critic.** Turn down that annoying roommate in your head that's constantly criticizing you. Let it go. Push it away.

2. **Manage your shock clock.** Build in down time between important activities. Allow yourself time to reflect and implement so that you're not overwhelmed by deadlines and multitasking.

3. **Define your word.** What makes you the real deal? Identify a word. Live it. Be it. Consistently—not just episodically.

4. **Identify your triggers.** What situations or people throw you off-center? Manage these conditions—don't just cope with them. Coping makes you a victim. Managing gives you control.

5. **Forget perfection; think excellence.** Give yourself permission to be your best *at this moment*, not the best of all time.

6. **Prepare for the positive.** Confidence is the expectation of a positive outcome in a specific situation. Prepare for positive outcomes, one situation at a time.

7. **Welcome feedback.** Fear of criticism drains your confidence and power. Build healthy humility by seeking feedback from people whom you respect.

8. **Focus on solutions, not problems.** Don't dissect a problem over and over again. Define the issue clearly and then present the best possible solutions.

9. **Seek commitment, not compliance.** Help people understand the *why* behind the *what* and you're far more likely to influence others and earn their buy-in.

10. **Fight EUI and TUI (e-mailing and texting under the influence).** If you're provoked, don't fire off a response immediately. Wait until your head clears so you can reflect and respond more carefully.

Identify the top three conditions or people that consistently knock your inner presence off-center:

Inner Presence Action Plan

1. _____

   _____

2. _____

   _____

3. _____

   _____

Three ways you plan to keep yourself centered when you find yourself in these situations or with these people:

1. _____

   _____

2. _____

   _____

3. _____

   _____

LAYER TWO: VERBAL PRESENCE

HOW YOU REVEAL YOUR MESSAGES

Transforming Rhetoric into Results

5

What Is Verbal Presence?
Managing Your Words

Quick—what pops into your head when you hear the phrase "verbal presence"? The deep, authoritative voice of James Earl Jones declaring, "Luke, I am your father" or "This . . . is CNN"? Perhaps it's the vocal chops of your favorite singer, like Adele, whose tones elicit a remarkable range of emotions—from longing to revenge. Maybe it's an impressive speaker like Sir Ken Robinson or the late Steve Jobs.

How you reveal your messages

All of these superstars have distinctive voices. And you may, too. But that's not what I mean by verbal presence. This may sound a bit confusing, but the sound produced by your vocal chords is part of your *outer* presence. Verbal presence is a different skill set, but it's equally make-or-break.

Confused? Let's start with a simple definition:

Verbal presence is how the world interprets your words.

87

Think of it as a transfer mechanism—a bridge between your inner and outer presence. It's your ability to effectively transfer the ideas and thoughts from inside your head to others, hopefully compelling them to act on what you say. It's also the capstone of the structure we've been building this whole time. You may be centered within yourself, and neither over- nor underestimate your abilities; you may come across as warm, approachable, and competent. But if you're not communicating your thoughts effectively, you still won't see your ideas put into action.

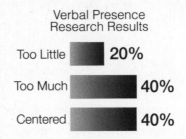

Verbal Presence
Research Results

Too Little ▮ 20%

Too Much ▮ 40%

Centered ▮ 40%

Presence Project participants were more likely to rate themselves as centered in verbal presence than in either of the other two layers. Yet, as shown above, 60 percent of participants still saw themselves as off-center.

How would you rate your own verbal presence?

Aim for a high signal-to-noise ratio

Having a centered verbal presence means having a high signal-to-noise ratio, which essentially means that you don't drown out your own messages because you're talking too much—or go unnoticed because you're being too quiet.

Counterintuitive as it may sound, verbal presence means *less rhetoric, more results.*

My coaching practice started with this concept. I wrote a book called *Talk Less, Say More* about a communication process that develops this skill set that I call *Connect, Convey, Convince.*®

Developing Verbal Presence

I will expand upon the *Connect, Convey, Convince* process in this book, because it's at the core of effective twenty-first-century communication. We're living in a distracted, demanding, impatient, impulsive society. People are quick to tune you out if they fail to find instant relevance in your message.

You probably feel this impatience, too. Have you noticed that you're saying or thinking "It's too long!" more and more frequently? Maybe you're talking about a movie. A meeting. A presentation. An e-mail. A voicemail. A book. (Hopefully you're not thinking that right now!)

Not less *filling*, less *filler*

I am a staunch ally of the "less is more" movement. But making communications shorter doesn't mean making them *less filling*. Instead, it means using *less filler*.

Developing a strong verbal presence will help you gain a reputation for being smart and respectful of other people's time. It will ensure that people answer your communications promptly and that they don't overlook or ignore your efforts. It will motivate people to put your ideas into action. It'll make you a more effective leader.

Before we move forward, please take a moment to refer back to your word cloud with a word in the Introduction. How do you want people to think of you? Do your communications support that?

Let's explore how to build your verbal presence in the following chapter.

Ready to learn more?

6

Centered
Verbal Presence

An hour into the meeting, the frustration level was palpable. Tim, a product manager at a consumer goods company, had just finished delivering what he thought was an irrefutable, iron-clad case to launch a new line.

Turning rhetoric into results

Senior leaders were not impressed.

I was sitting quietly in the back of the room and knew exactly how the CEO, Dean, would respond. "Where's the profit potential?" he challenged the product manager. "Look, Tim, I can see you're passionate about this idea. But if there's a compelling business case here, you've hidden it well."

As communicator-in-chief, Dean spends 80 percent of his time in meetings. All too often, he's on the receiving end of half-baked ideas. Employees throw everything—too much, in fact—at Dean in a desire to win his approval. So he's forced to extract the critical details that will help him make the decisions that weigh heavily on corporate profits. He has to listen well, zero in on the details that connect the current idea to the company's big picture, and deliver his verdict—and the reason for it—clearly.

But day in and day out, employees like Tim fail to hit the core issues that would persuade Dean and his executive team to give them the green light. Dean has to evaluate these pitches and respond to them in a way that will teach the Tims of the world to do better next time.

It'd be easy for Dean to sit in that meeting, decide that Tim's idea won't make the cut, and conclude that he's just wasted an hour. But Dean is a better communicator than that. He knows how to give an hour something that's known as "the Einstein treatment."

Albert Einstein was quoted as having said that if he had an hour to solve a problem, he'd spend the first 55 minutes understanding the problem—and the last five minutes solving it.

Be passionately curious

That's what people with centered verbal presence do. They're passionately curious, just like Einstein. They don't run their mouths without running their brains first.

Think of the most powerful communicators you've ever encountered—people who changed your mind, touched your heart, or moved you to action. Think of people in the public eye whom you strongly associate with a single, clear message. All of the individuals you're envisioning have a centered verbal presence. Like Dean, they know how to cut through the noise to get to the heart of an issue or idea.

When I think of what a centered verbal presence looks like, I think of someone like American business magnate and investment expert Warren Buffett. He's long been known for his simple, on-point style. His yearly letter to shareholders is probably the most-read annual report in the corporate world—and not just because of his financial success. It's also because he's so straightforward about what caused whatever success or failure he's discussing, and because he uses clear, colorful stories to make his points. You don't need an MBA to decipher his message. He's not trying to impress you with his knowledge of analyses; he's just trying to help you *understand the facts.*

Buffett brought that on-point style to his entry into the political debate in 2012 over the divide between America's haves and have-nots. He presented his argument for higher taxes on the rich in the same plainspoken way he's always explained his multinational conglomerate Berkshire Hathaway's ups and downs. He focused on broad themes such as *fairness* (the rich shouldn't pay less than the middle class, he reasoned) and kept

What Centered Looks Like

the numbers in what eventually became known as the "Buffett Rule" easy to remember—a tax of at least 30 percent on incomes over $1 million.

You might disagree with his argument or the logic behind it, but you'll certainly understand it—and remember it. And that's because it's simple and congruent with his down-to-earth personal style.

I also think of Dr. Jill Bolte Taylor when I envision someone with remarkable verbal presence. If you've seen her powerful TED Talk, you'll know that while she's not as polished and slick as some other TED presenters, she delivers a powerful message that could change your life.

Dr. Bolte Taylor is a "naked presenter." Not naked as in without clothes, rather naked as in without pretense. She doesn't slip into formal presentation mode or try to impress the audience with medical jargon. She explains her research in terms anyone can understand: "We were essentially mapping the microcircuitry of the brain, which cells are communicating with which cells, with which chemicals."

Polished, but not slick   Yes, she has some unique delivery quirks, but she's not trying to be slick. She shows up as herself, and you embrace her as the authentic professional that she is.

Dr. Bolte Taylor's authenticity demonstrates that she's got a centered outer presence. But her talk wouldn't have the same impact if she didn't also have a centered verbal presence. She leads her audience toward a simple but powerful call to action: she wants you to choose to live more from the "ecstatically connected" right side of your brain. Everything in her talk points toward this conclusion. She knows where she wants to take people, and she designed her speech as a journey leading straight to that point.

One of the most centered communicators I've seen speak recently is Gabrielle Giffords. As a politician, Giffords had long fought for her constituents. But it's her personal fight after she was shot in the head while speaking to constituents at a "Congress on Your Corner" event in 2011 that has influenced the nation.

Giffords's sheer determination and upbeat attitude inspire millions. The damage to her language pathways limits her vocabulary, and she struggles to form sentences. Yet she makes it crystal clear that she's committed to rebuilding the connections in both her brain and her community. She doesn't say much, but she chooses her words carefully. It's impossible to not feel moved while watching her speak.

Giffords's story—that inner resolve trumps evil acts—connects with everyone. And she proves that a short, well-crafted message delivered with passion can be far more influential than a lengthy speech.

Are You Centered?

It's pretty easy to tell if your verbal presence was centered after you've conveyed your message simply by measuring the results of your communications. Did people put your ideas into action? Did they do so enthusiastically, rather than just because you're the boss? If so, you've probably been centered.

It's a little trickier to know if you're centered in the moment, and to make sure you will be centered for your *next* big moment. But there are some signs to watch for. If you're centered, you will know:

- When to talk and when to listen.
- When to ask questions and when to make decisions.
- When to challenge assumptions and when to accept conclusions.
- What you want your audience to do and how to guide them to the desired outcome.

Start with your ideal outcome

That last point is perhaps the most important. Once you've determined the goal of your communication—whether it's a conversation, a meeting, a presentation, or a big keynote speech—you're already on your way to becoming centered. Understanding your desired outcome will help you ask the right questions, listen for the right details, and identify a satisfactory conclusion. It'll also help you craft your message, stick to the essential points, and move your audience to a specific action.

While some people revel in public speaking, there are plenty who avoid it (or attempt to) at all costs. And that's okay; you don't have to love the limelight to have a centered verbal presence. But you *do* have to be willing to step up and speak.

I recently worked with a client who needed to find this balance. Priya's company was preparing for its annual conference, when 2,500 men and women from their sales force around the globe would gather to learn about the new product lineup. As the head of marketing, she was responsible for organizing the event, but she usually let folks from the sales team make the main stage speeches. She didn't like being the center of attention, so she happily ceded the spotlight.

This year's event was going to be different, however. The company had a particularly full slate of innovative new products. So Priya decided that instead of spreading the trade-show part of the event out over two floors of the conference center like they usually did, they'd set up the booths in the back of the main ballroom. She wanted to emphasize that this year was different, and put these exciting new products front and center.

"You should give the kickoff speech," I told her.

"Oh, I never do that," she said. "I'm not in sales."

"That's exactly why you *should* speak." I replied. "This conference is different from anything you've done before. It's an opportunity to show the team they're not going to hear the same old pitches they've always heard."

Priya still didn't look convinced, so I tried a new approach. "What's your ideal outcome for this conference?"

She answered immediately. "I want our sales force to open up to me. They're the ones out in the field with the customers, but they don't give us enough honest feedback back at the world headquarters. I want them to tell me what problems we need to fix, and what opportunities we're missing. I want them to talk to me!"

Communicate to add value

"OK, how many people do you want to hear from?"

"Ten," Priya said.

"Too low! Let's aim higher."

"Twenty."

"Still too low," I said.

"Okay, 25; that's 1 percent of the attendees. If 1 percent of our audience tells me something that could boost our profitability, I would be *thrilled*."

With that goal in mind, we were able to design a show-stopping talk that Priya felt comfortable, even *happy* delivering. In the end, her reluctance to take center stage became an asset. She wanted to keep the focus on the company's new products, so her crack communications team had her surprise the audience by popping up in the back of the room where the trade show was set up, instead of walking onto the main stage like every other speaker. We kept her talk short; though they'd initially allotted an hour, she spoke for only 10 concise minutes. She focused on the new products and then she made her appeal, asking the attendees for honest feedback from the field.

I watched proudly as she delivered her terrific talk before I had to catch a flight to my next assignment. Imagine my surprise to get a text from her the next day saying, "Connie, I didn't get 25 people."

"I can't believe it!" I texted back.

"I stopped counting at *200*," she wrote back.

Priya got that amazing result because of her centered verbal presence. She had a clear purpose for her talk. At past conferences, the introductory speakers hadn't said much beyond "Welcome" and "Have a great week." But Priya knew what she wanted and asked for it directly. She had a high signal-to-noise ratio because she *connected* with what her audience wanted and valued, *conveyed* the right amount of information, and *convinced* them to take specific action.

When you have a centered verbal presence, you identify your ideal outcome from the beginning. You set metrics for success and you design your communication to get you there. You're communicating to *add something*, not just to be seen speaking.

Priya's speech got fantastic results. She came back from that conference with clear ideas about how to develop more new products, solve common customer issues, and improve customer relationships. If you can develop a centered verbal presence, you'll get results, too.

Traits of Centered Presence

Priya and Dean have a few things in common with great communicators like Dr. Jill Bolte Taylor, Warren Buffett, and Gabby Giffords—besides great results.

Here are a few characteristics of people with a centered verbal presence:

They deliver compelling messages. You want to take full advantage of the time you're allotted. Dr. Bolte Taylor didn't use her 18 minutes on stage at the TED Conference to give her audience a simple summary of her research. She used her time to persuade people to think about their place in the world in a completely new way. Attention is precious in today's fractured, fast-paced world. When you have it—either a single person's or an entire audience's—use that opportunity to deliver the most important message you can.

They balance input and output. If you're the only one talking, you're not centered—and the same is true if you never talk at all. Aim for a balance between contributing to the conversation and hearing what other participants have to say. For Priya, that meant keeping her talk short so that her audience would really hear her key message: the appeal for feedback. It also meant making herself available for the more than 200 people who responded to that appeal.

They listen well. Listening isn't just what you do when you don't happen to be talking; *listening is the desire to hear.* You can't just be waiting for your turn to talk, or "on guard" for any attacks on your ideas when someone else is speaking. You have to *want* to hear what the other person has to say. You might even consider taking notes; it may help you stay focused. Try summarizing a colleague's point before you go on to make your own. Your own contributions will be more thoughtful and on target if they take others' ideas into account.

They refine others' input. A centered communicator helps *everyone* make the best possible contribution. Instead of trying to prove a colleague wrong or score points off them when they're off-target, help them get closer to the mark. Dean could have just thrown Tim out of the executive suite when his pitch missed the mark; instead, he tried to *show* Tim how and where he went wrong. Helping your colleague make their most valuable contributions possible will elevate your entire team, and ultimately help you do your own best work.

They're candid, but not abrasive. Dean had to reject Tim's pitch. But that didn't mean he had to put Tim himself down. While he didn't sugarcoat his rejection, he did make sure Tim knew he appreciated his work. Delivering a clear message is always important, but it's even more important when you've got to give someone bad news. Your goal should be to get them to focus on the *content*, not the tone of your message.

They start with the big picture. Dean didn't waste time picking apart the design or the name of the new product line Tim was proposing. He got straight to the point by asking: where's the business case? Details matter, of course; but if you don't have the big picture in mind, you won't focus on the right details. Start with the macro and work your way to the micro. It'll help you ask the right questions and waste no time getting to the point when you speak.

They know what's at stake. Priya knew the feedback she could get from the distributors would help her improve relationships with her customers. She knew what was at stake in her opening remarks, and it wasn't making herself look good or making the attendees feel welcome. It was her company's reputation and financial health. The knowledge of what was at stake helped her focus her message.

They share "why." Once you've determined what's at stake, share that knowledge with your audience. Remember, you're aiming for commitment, not compliance. Your audience is more likely to put your ideas into action if they know the reasons behind your proposals.

They deliver color commentary, not play-by-play. Dr. Bolte Taylor doesn't just tell her audience what happened to her during her speech; she tells them *exactly how she felt* at each moment. Even if you're not telling a first-person story, you can add motivation, reasons, and emotions to what you're saying. Warren Buffett's op-ed wouldn't have had as much impact if he hadn't grounded his message in the idea of fairness. Add color and texture to your messages to help people remember them.

Their words carry weight. Of course, many people opposed Buffett's tax proposal; but everyone took it seriously. Other pundits crunched the numbers on how much revenue such a tax would raise, debated whether it would inhibit entrepreneurship, and so on. Even the president started talking about the "Buffett Rule." When someone with a centered verbal presence speaks, people listen—because they're delivering a clear, compelling message in a straightforward, succinct way.

They know what they want. You won't achieve your ideal outcome unless you know what it is. When you have a goal in mind, you can design your message to lead your audience in that direction. So, design your message by starting with your close. Ask yourself, "What, specifically, do I want my audience to do when I'm done talking?" Once you've settled on this critical but often overlooked element, then go back and develop the opening and middle of your communication.

How to Stay Centered

Centered communication is situational—which means you have to keep working at it. Every time you begin a conversation or start to craft a new message, you've got to think about eliminating filler, being candid, and staying focused on the goal of your communication.

And that goal will vary, depending on the situation. For instance—in one of the biggest moments of my client Justin's career, his goal was to be a good wingman. His company's CEO and other senior leaders were flying to Wall Street for a meeting with important analysts. They brought Justin, an expert on a promising new product line, along to help them prepare.

This was a huge opportunity for Justin, since it was a rare chance for him to get close to the CEO. He knew he had to strike the right tone. In this case, the appropriate level of verbal presence was to play a supporting role. He had to be ready to answer questions clearly, but without interjecting himself in an attempt to get attention.

At dinner the night before the big meeting, the CEO, CFO, and the Senior Vice President of Sales were discussing a legacy product line that Justin's project would partially replace. The CEO asked about the latest customer survey, trying to figure out how to address the issue if an analyst wanted to know whether they'd eventually phase out the older product. The head of sales said customers were still very happy with the older product and would likely continue to buy it at a lower price point.

Then the CEO turned to Justin. "Your team has been studying this. What does your research say?"

This was a delicate moment. On the one hand, it was Justin's big chance to impress the senior leaders with a clear and accurate answer to an important question. He knew the customer surveys showed that satisfaction with the older product was declining, and the new product would likely become a replacement for it, not simply an alternative. On the other hand, he also risked alienating the head of sales by pointing out that he was wrong.

Justin explained the survey results, and he also gave the SVP of sales a way to save face by saying, "You might be referring to another survey we did last month. I'll send you both studies as soon as we get back from dinner."

Justin handled this delicate situation perfectly. He was candid, but polite. Both the CEO and the head of sales were able to hear what he said because he remained focused on giving everyone the information that they needed—not on making himself look good (or anyone else look bad).

Know the role you need to play   Verbal presence, like the other two forms of presence, depends on the situation. That means you need to know what role you need to play at any particular moment, and you need to be agile.

Sometimes that means taking the spotlight, and sometimes it means doing more listening than talking. Think about it: You don't get up in the middle of the sermon and start preaching when you're sitting in church, do you? (I hope not.) You're there to absorb, not to lead. If you're in a supporting role, own it. Play it well.

Justin's role at that dinner was to help the CEO reach the best decision. He didn't sugarcoat his answer or hold back information for fear of offending the head of sales, but he also didn't turn that moment into a power play. He stayed focused on contributing to the conversation.

He was also *decisive*. He knew that there were two viewpoints on the issue, and he stood up for the side he believed in. Holding back or censoring your opinion doesn't help your organization. If you're there to support your team, support them! Say what you know to be true, and say it candidly.

Focusing on your goal will always help you stay centered. Ask yourself, why am I attending this meeting? Why am I giving this presentation? Keep thinking about that goal, and you'll find it helps you keep your communications on point. Less noise, more signal: that's what a centered verbal presence is all about.

....

INFLUENCING THE MEDIA

A reporter wants to interview you. Your mind is racing—what will he ask me? Will he edit my comments or otherwise make me look foolish?

I spent 20 years as a television journalist interviewing thousands of leaders. Some were terrific. Sadly, many blew it. Wordiness, nervousness, lack of preparation, or arrogance sabotaged their opportunity to shine.

A media interview is just that—an opportunity. You're given a platform to deliver specific messages that can bolster your organization and your leadership. Here are three techniques for mastering your media messages:

1. **Anticipate their questions.**

   Make a list of three questions that you'd *like* to be asked—and three questions that you would *least* like to be asked. The three questions you want to answer are your key messages, which you'll learn how to develop in a moment. But first you've got to tackle the questions you don't want asked. A good reporter will probe. She may be assigned to uncover exactly what you want to keep a lid on. Flesh out answers to these crucial questions before you meet the media.

2. **Bridge to the positive.**

   Bridging is a communication technique to transition smoothly from unwelcome questions to positive answers. Think of it as connective tissue. To bridge successfully, use the ABC method: Answer, Bridge, Context. For example:

   Reporter's Question: "What was your return on sales last quarter?"

   Answer: "For competitive reasons, I can't share a specific number . . ."

Bridge: ". . . but let me put this into perspective . . ."

Context: ". . . we shattered our goals and the future is very promising."

If you bridge to a message that's meaty or colorful enough, most reporters will be satisfied. You'll dodge a bullet—and deliver a positive punch.

3. **Hone three sound bites.**

Ah, yes, I sense your resistance. You're thinking that sound bites are glib one-liners. Not this type. Solid sound bites are a potent tool for delivering key messages. Think of them as x-rays. They're magnetic ideas or thoughts, honed to their essence, that energize both reporters and audiences. In today's impatient, distracted world, it's imperative that you deliver quick messages that stick.

How do you develop sound bites? Write down the three questions that you'd like to be asked and then write your answers. At first, your responses will likely be wordy or confusing. Don't let the curse of knowledge derail you—simplicity is a complex business. Sharpen each key message until it's one sentence. You can expand on it after the reporter responds. Using this approach, you'll find that sound bites can truly be sound answers.

One last thing. Don't fall for "off the record." There's no such thing. Ever.

7

Too Little
The Mouse

too little
"The Mouse"

Real Deal

On Point

"I feel like I made a mistake," Keisha told me. **Tongue-tied** We were sitting outside on a beautiful fall day, **with the boss** surrounded by laughing, chatting students criss-crossing the bustling, elite university campus, but Keisha didn't seem to notice any of it. Her coffee sat untouched on the table. "I wish I could just go back to the foundation—but they've already filled my old job."

"So why did you leave in the first place? Why did you take *this* position?" I asked, gently.

"This university made a big difference in my life. I worked hard to get here and it gave me so many opportunities. When they called and offered me a position, I felt like I'd have a chance to create those opportunities for today's students," Keisha said.

"So why can't you say that to the school's potential donors? What's holding you back?"

This was literally the million-dollar question—actually, more like a multimillion-dollar question. Keisha's alma mater had recruited her to play a key role as the head of the development department. She'd previously worked for several nonprofits and had increased the fundraising of all the organizations she'd served.

Until now. In her current position, Keisha found herself tongue-tied in board meetings and consumed with stage fright at alumni events. She couldn't seem to come up with the kinds of innovative ideas that had made her so successful in the past. She was missing fundraising targets for the first time in her career. The board was frustrated, and she was miserable.

Something about this new role had turned Keisha into *The Mouse*—someone with far too little verbal presence. And if we couldn't find a way to make her voice heard, she might end up quitting—or losing—this exciting new job.

What Too Little Looks Like

For Keisha, having too little verbal presence meant not speaking up at all. But that's not the only way to be a Mouse. Remember, having a centered verbal presence means speaking up in the appropriate way, at the appropriate time, to influence your audience. It means turning rhetoric into results.

When the "pink slime" scandal hit the media in the spring of 2012, Beef Products Inc. (BPI)—the main producer of what's formally known as "lean finely textured beef"—didn't stay silent. But the way they spoke up didn't get results, either. They created websites to fight the "myths" about the product, took out an ad in the *Wall Street Journal* complaining about the media's "campaign of lies and deceit," and recruited government allies to tout the product's safety. But despite this flurry of activity, the company still had to shut down several plants because demand for "pink slime" had plunged so sharply.

BPI's mistake was that they allowed the media to set the terms of the conversation. Instead of telling their own story about their products, they were backed into a corner—and then all they could do was try to tell a story about how "pink slime" isn't as bad as it sounds. They also dropped the social media ball. If they'd been tracking online conversations carefully, they could have spotted the "pink slime" story cropping up on blogs before it hit ABC News.

Don't allow others to define you

BPI showed too little verbal presence because the company didn't speak up proactively to tell their own authentic story. Had they engaged in more open communication earlier about *all* of their products, they might have defused this PR disaster before it started.

Individuals can run into the same kind of trouble. If you don't speak up and share your ideas, claim appropriate credit for your hard work, and define your message for your colleagues and your audience, you'll end up letting someone else define you. You'll be *The Mouse*.

Following the explosion of British Petroleum's Deepwater Horizon drilling rig and the resulting oil spill in 2010, BP CEO Tony Hayward wasn't exactly shy about speaking up, either. But he showed too little verbal presence by not *thinking* before he spoke—and by not saying enough of the kinds of things his audience needed to hear.

What does your audience need to hear?

Hayward's most infamous comment began as an attempt to prove he understood the gravity of the situation. With TV cameras rolling, he first said, "We're sorry for the massive disruption" the oil spill has caused. But then he went on: "There's no one who wants this over more than I do. I would like my life back."

Hayward's blunt, off-the-cuff speaking style had previously been regarded as one of his strengths. But in this case, rehearsing his remarks would have helped him convey that he was indeed the thoughtful, contrite person his audience wanted to see. It would have helped him to avoid appearing as less than totally committed to fixing the problems his company had caused for other people. He didn't think enough about his audience, and he didn't tailor his remarks to the situation. He became a squeaking, complaining Mouse instead of the strong leader his company needed him to be.

Remember, presence is situational. A style that works when everything is going well won't be appropriate when you have to own up to a major mistake. You can't present to the board in the same style you'd use to chat with your colleagues. You have to stay focused on what your audience needs to hear, or you'll show up as less than they need you to be. You'll become a Mouse—and I don't mean Mickey. This version is a lot less lovable.

If you have trouble speaking up in meetings or avoid big presentations like the plague, it's pretty easy to self-diagnose a low verbal presence. But sometimes the signs are a little more subtle—and you may not even be aware of the toll the problem is taking on your career.

Here are some characteristics that people with too little verbal presence exhibit:

Traits of the Mouse

They fail to contribute. This doesn't have to mean staying completely quiet. It may mean fulfilling the letter of their job description but not following the spirit of it, by holding back a new idea or failing to speak up about a problem because they're afraid to criticize a colleague. BPI spoke up in the "pink slime" example, but they didn't contribute anything new to the conversation: they just responded to what the media were saying. The bottom line is: you don't show up as yourself when you don't contribute your honest opinion—and you don't convey enough verbal presence.

They avoid conflict or judgment. Inner presence issues can contribute to verbal presence problems. An anxious person who's afraid that others will judge or find him or her wanting—or a conflict-avoidant person who doesn't want to openly disagree with a colleague—will show up with too little verbal presence. But not speaking up, whatever the reason, means shirking your duty to your organization.

They're undervalued. The president at Keisha's university was starting to wonder if he'd made a mistake in hiring her. She was a talented fundraiser with a true passion for the school, but all he could see was someone who wasn't pulling her weight. People with low verbal presence sabotage their own careers because they don't speak up with their best ideas and show up as their best selves.

They're frustrated. Keisha wasn't happy, either; after all, she was thinking of leaving her new job. Many people with low verbal presence are all too aware that they're not doing their best work. They know they're not advancing the way they want to, and know they could be contributing more. But something's holding them back; something about the situation they're in is making them show up as something less.

They're stuck in their own heads. "Nobody wants this over more than I do" wasn't just a boneheaded thing to say on camera—it was a perfect example of the Mouse's self-absorbed nature. If Hayward hadn't been so focused on his own experience, he would have been able to say what his audience needed to hear.

How to Increase Low Verbal Presence

Keisha wasn't the only one on the development team having trouble speaking up. Her second-in-command, Karen, had just blown a big opportunity. She'd met with a potential major donor, a recent immigrant who had started a business in the area and was looking for ways to make a name for himself in the community. Karen got him to give the school $10,000. Not bad—until they heard a few days later that he'd given a local hospital $10 million.

Losing a chance to collect $10 million is a big mistake, but it was actually fairly easy to fix. Karen had gone into the conversation focused on her own nervousness about asking for a really big donation. She told the donor what the *minimum* donation was and left it at that, because she didn't want to seem pushy. But this guy *wanted* to make a big gift. He wanted his name on a building. The university could have given that to him—but he gave his $10 million to the organization and the person who *asked for it*.

Karen's mistake was thinking too much about herself. Ten million dollars sounded like an unrealistic goal to her. She didn't want this guy to think she was off her rocker. If she'd thought more about *him*—about what he likely *wanted* as a business owner who was trying to make a big splash in the community—she probably would have offered him the chance to get exactly what he wanted by giving her the millions.

Keisha's problem was a variation on the same theme. It became clear as we talked that she was a little nervous about whether her skills would translate to the academic world. The university's donor profile was slightly different from the profile for the foundations she'd worked for in the past. Plus, she'd previously been advocating for other people—underserved members of the community.

In this situation, her biggest asset was her *own* story. She just had to find the courage to tell it.

I coached Keisha's staff on doing deeper donor research and figuring out how to push past their fears to make bigger asks. I worked with Keisha on how she needed to contribute, too—by learning something I call "planned spontaneity." Before any meeting, she needed to look at the agenda and write down a few things she could contribute. Doing this exercise helped her face the fact that she *did* have good ideas to share; she'd just been too nervous to share them in real time.

Think conversation, not presentation

I also encouraged Keisha to see the process of speaking in front of the board differently—not as a presentation, but as a *conversation*. Presentations gave her stage fright, especially as a newcomer on this team. But as a fundraiser, she was basically a professional conversationalist. Once we shifted her focus from her own nerves to making connections with her new board, she warmed up, and she started speaking up.

Does Keisha's story sound familiar? Do you ever show up as less than yourself?

TIPS

If you've been lacking verbal presence for any reason, here are some tips that should help you show up and speak up:

Put it on paper. This strategy helped Keisha. Her notes prompted her to speak up in meetings where she might have stayed silent. Seeing something in writing lets you review your idea and fix it if necessary. An idea that stays in your head helps no one. Write it down, make it real, and get it out there.

Avoid crutch words. I'm not just talking about "like" or "um." Words like "actually" or phrases like "be that as it may" or "as it were" can be empty filler, too. Using words as time-fillers diminishes your authority. Learn to pause when you're thinking of what to say next instead of stalling for time with filler words. Get a friend to help you. Train yourself out of the crutch word habit.

Pose positive questions. If you're having trouble speaking up, try asking some thoughtful questions. You'll be making a contribution without putting yourself on the spot. Remember to put a positive spin on your questions. Because it takes a lot more brainpower to process negative questions, they slow people down. Positive questions, on the other hand, prompt your colleagues to find solutions. Instead of asking, "Why didn't we meet our fund-raising goal this quarter?" try asking, "How can we improve our process for next quarter?"

Master the power pause. Increasing your verbal presence doesn't just mean talking more. It means communicating more effectively. Use pauses to underscore your most important points. A break in speaking signals to your audience that they've just heard something significant. Use this technique sparingly so you don't dilute its impact.

Think like an analyst. When you do speak up, make sure you add color and analysis to your comments. People won't remember a dry data point unless you connect it to the bigger story you're trying to tell. Don't just recite the sales figures for the quarter—analyze them. What went well or poorly? What's behind these numbers?

Focus on serving others. Thinking carefully about what your audience wants and needs to hear will do several things for you. First, it'll help you get over any nervousness that's holding you back, by shifting your focus away from yourself. If your mind tends to go blank in meetings, this will help you come up with things to contribute. And it'll compel you to craft a focused message that people will remember.

How to Manage a Mouse

Do you have a Keisha or a pink slime representative on your team? Whether their problem is nerves or simply saying the wrong thing, putting them on the spot in public won't help.

Here are some strategies that will *help you boost the verbal presence of The Mouse in your office*:

Ask specific questions. Help them see the contribution they can make to the conversation. Ask a question that will point them in the right direction. Instead of saying something vague like, "Jim, can you weigh in on this?" try something more like, "Jim, can you share some of the lessons learned from the software implementation process last year?"

Prod them to prepare. Unprepared speakers are prone to gaffes, while unprepared meeting attendees often stay quiet because they think they have nothing to say. Offer to help your colleague prepare for a big presentation. If you're a team leader, ask them to come to meetings prepared to speak on a specific topic. Help them break complex subjects into chunks.

Cheer them on. When your colleague does contribute to the conversation or deliver a strong presentation, give them some positive feedback. We humans are pretty simple animals. We tend to repeat actions we're praised for. Praise your quiet colleague for speaking up, and he'll be more likely to do it again.

Enforce order. The Mouse can easily be overwhelmed by *a Motor Mouth* (see Chapter 8). Make sure your team doesn't drown out the quieter voices amongst its members. If you can, make rules against interrupting in meetings and *enforce them*. When someone does interrupt a colleague, politely but firmly ask that the first speaker get a chance to finish their point.

Give specific feedback. Let a colleague know if she's showing up as less than herself by getting defensive or saying the wrong thing. Be diplomatic, but direct. Most people don't really know how others hear their words. Your colleague may need a wake-up call that will prompt her to tailor her messages more appropriately.

Remind them to speak up. If your colleague doesn't proactively share the right information— or, like Karen, simply seems to forget to account for her audience's needs—speak up. Say something like, "I think the board needs to hear more about the results of your research; it could change their decision," or "I'm not sure you've shared enough with our customers about the difference between this model and the old one." If you prompt her to focus on her audience, she's more likely to speak up effectively.

Tony Hayward may be out as BP's CEO, but Keisha and Karen are still doing important work for their prestigious university. Better preparation and a shift in focus helped them learn to speak up effectively and share the things their audiences wanted to hear. It can take some work to increase verbal presence, but it can definitely be done.

....

WHAT'S YOUR CRUTCH WORD?

Ever had a broken leg or ankle? If so, you probably wielded a set of crutches as a temporary mobility aid.

Sadly, crutch words are neither temporary nor helpful. They're annoying. The verbal placeholders that frequently roll off your tongue clutter up your communications and may drive your listeners to start counting. (They may even inspire a drinking game or two.)

It's easy to poke fun at someone else's classic guttural fillers such as "um" or "uh"—but is it possible that you're peppering your sentences with other go-to words that dilute your impact? Words that you didn't even realize had crept into your lexicon?

Here's a Top 10 list of frequently used crutch words and phrases that my clients say they'd like to eliminate from their vocabularies:

Top Ten Crutch Words

1. At the end of the day . . .
2. Literally . . .
3. Actually . . .
4. Basically . . .
5. That being said . . .
6. It is what it is . . .
7. Honestly . . .
8. For what it's worth . . .
9. As a matter of fact . . .
10. For all intents and purposes . . .

What's your crutch of choice? Perhaps one or more of these words and phrases have gotten lodged in your brain and come out of your mouth on an all-too-frequent basis. Are you aware of any hackneyed expressions or aging metaphors that need to go?

The first step to getting rid of them is awareness. Peruse your e-mail outbox to see if your sent e-mails are littered with crutch words or phrases. That's a private method. Another technique is to ask a friend or colleague to make you aware of your crutch words and monitor you for overuse. There's a third technique if you happen to have teenagers: ask your kids what crutch words you overuse. Your teenagers are always happy to tell you what's wrong with you!

Awareness is key

For all intents and purposes, at the end of the day, ultimately all that matters is basically that you rid yourself of these sentence suckers. *It is what it is.* That being said, for what it's worth, it's stealing your power. *Honestly. As a matter of fact,* I think we're done here. *Literally.*

....

8

Too Much
The Motor Mouth

too much
**"Motor
Mouth"**

Michel had been a great college business profes- **Boring others**
sor. He had no trouble delivering a three-hour **to tears**
lecture; given his deep expertise and careful preparation for each class, he could easily have talked for
twice as long. He was particularly beloved by his
introductory students because he was so good at
breaking down complex concepts. He'd start
almost every lecture with a reminder of basic
business principles and then build from there.

Unfortunately, he wasn't in a lecture hall anymore. Michel was now the president of a division

123

of a major global corporation. And the qualities that had made him successful in his former field were giving him significant trouble in his new one.

"We know he's smart," said the board member who called me for help. "Trust me, we *definitely* know that. But he's boring us to tears! We can't go on like this much longer."

Michel was drowning the board in information overload. He knew he'd been hired as the new president primarily to capitalize on growth opportunities in developing markets. But instead of showing the board one chart of the projected growth, he'd show them *seven*—and he'd spend 15 minutes explaining each. He'd drone on and on—one grueling detail after another—and then circle the wagons to share even more information.

The board members were experienced business leaders, not the college freshmen Michel was used to talking to. They didn't need to see his math. And they'd tried to tell him he was talking too much, usually by asking more advanced questions to try to hurry him past the basics. But Michel would just keep talking. The CEO would even say things like "OK, got it!" But Michel would just keep talking. They finally started scheduling his reports at the very end of their meetings, to try to keep him from eating everyone else's time. But Michel would just keep talking. He'd be following the board members out of the room, still talking.

"I've studied this field for years," Michel told me. "I just want to make sure we're making the best possible decisions based on all the available information."

"But Michel, you're overexplaining things to the board," I said. "They feel that you're hogging too much time on the agenda."

"I want them to see how I came up with my recommendations," he said.

Michel had a lot of reasons for delivering these lengthy monologues. But I eventually managed to convince him to see these meetings as *dialogues*, rather than monologues. He learned to present his point of view and one or two key data points, and then let the board ask him for any more details they wanted.

He learned to turn his monologues into *conversations*.

What Too Much Looks Like

If you've ever watched the Academy Awards, you've definitely seen a few examples of *The Motor Mouth* in action. At least the Oscars have a system for controlling excessive verbal presence: the music gradually swells until the chatterbox takes the hint and leaves the stage! (We members of the professional world aren't so lucky.)

You've probably seen it happen enough times that it seems like just part of the show; but let's take a moment to think about the kinds of acceptance speeches that tend to get Oscar winners "played off" the stage. Sometimes someone goes on a lengthy political rant. Sometimes they pull out a creased piece of paper and start reading off the names of everyone they've ever met. Sometimes they take up too much time trying to explain how much they respect their fellow nominees and then they're scrambling to squeeze in their thank-yous.

What's the common factor? They're not thinking about *what their audience wants to hear*. The Oscars is a three-hour event. Each individual who makes it up to that stage to accept a statue is experiencing one of the greatest moments of his or her life. But the hard truth is that for the audience, it's just one of about 50 almost identical speeches they're going to hear that evening. The audience wants to see the winners' excitement, and hear heartfelt gratitude; they just don't want to hear it for very long.

Centered *verbal* presence starts with a centered *inner* presence. If you're too focused on yourself, you won't be able to craft a compelling speech or make a clear point in a meeting—because you won't be thinking about what your audience wants or needs to hear.

Are you trying to prove your worth?

That's what happened to Michel. The longer we worked together, the clearer it became that his motor-mouth tendencies stemmed from a desire to prove himself to others. He wanted the board to know how smart he was, how deep his expertise was, and how much he'd studied the questions before the company. He wanted to make sure that they took his years of experience in academia seriously. He wanted his hard work to be visible.

But Michel needed to learn that while they of course *did* value his expertise, the business world values *brevity* as well. He needed to put himself in his audience's seats and really think about what information they needed to hear—and what he could leave unexplained. He needed to start with his goal—getting the board to sign off on his recommendations—and then design his time with the board to achieve that goal.

Have you ever been cut off by a voicemail system and had to call back to finish your message? Do you often get the last slot on the meeting agenda? Do people tend to call you at the end of the day, or after business hours, expecting (probably even *hoping*) to get your voicemail? If so, you're probably talking too much. Keep reading to see if you should really diagnose yourself with a motor mouth problem.

If any of this sounds uncomfortably familiar, you're not alone. A great number of my coaching clients tend to talk too much. Many of us are having trouble finding the sweet spot in today's fast-paced, impatient world.

Traits of a Motor Mouth

Here are some common traits of people with excessive verbal presence. Do you see yourself here?

They want their efforts to be visible. This is the inner presence origin of many verbal presence problems. It was certainly Michel's Achilles' heel. He was so concerned about showing the board how carefully he was studying the key questions that he didn't have any bandwidth left to focus on his audience's needs. He didn't design his presentations with them in mind, and he didn't pay enough attention to the (eventually not so subtle) hints they were giving him that they'd had enough.

They're seen as a blowhard or arrogant. Unfortunately, trying too hard to impress people almost always backfires. Remember, humans are incredibly good at picking up on unconscious cues. Your audience can tell if you're talking to puff yourself up. You know a blowhard when you see one, don't you? So does everyone else.

They prevent others from contributing. Motor Mouths tend to interrupt their colleagues, talk over them, or eat up their time on the agenda. They push their colleagues' ideas to the sidelines in favor of their own. And their team's work suffers for it.

They don't learn anything. It's not just the company's problem if people don't hear potentially great ideas because a Motor Mouth is talking too loud. It's the talker's problem, too. Think about Michel: as proud as he should have been of his academic experience, he didn't have as much business world experience as the folks on the board. His lengthy monologues kept him from hearing some great questions from his board— and kept him from learning from *their* experience.

They dominate. Motor Mouths tend to get compliance, not commitment. Because they shut out their colleagues' questions and ideas, they don't truly convince anyone to go along with their plans; they just get people to nod and (maybe) smile. They'll find that colleagues implement their plans slowly and reluctantly, because they haven't taken the time to listen and learn from the people who are executing the job.

They cause rumbles. Nobody likes being excluded from a conversation. When Motor Mouths work on teams, they can create conflict because they upset or offend their colleagues. They may steamroll a colleague in a meeting only to hear complaints later on—or be surprised when someone who's been interrupted one too many times snaps back.

They often reveal things they wish they hadn't. In some cases, Motor Mouths may blurt out or allude to something they should have kept confidential simply because they haven't given careful, advance thought to what they're going to say. In other cases, they may reveal unconscious thoughts or feelings they intended to keep hidden. If you dash off an e-mail without thinking or speak off the cuff without preparing or practicing, you're more likely to reveal your anxiety, your narcissism, your dislike of a colleague—or something else you'll later regret and could have avoided if you'd centered yourself before speaking.

They're easily distracted. Being a centered communicator is like going to the grocery store with a list. You know what you're there for, and you move quickly to fill your cart with the necessary items. Having too much verbal presence, on the other hand, is like shopping without a list. You wander the aisles aimlessly and stop every few seconds to consider buying a dozen different brightly colored packages of snack food. If you don't know the purpose of your communication— if you don't have a plan—you're more likely to get distracted or sidetracked.

They can't see the forest for the trees. The other problem with shopping without a list is that you might get home and realize you still don't have anything you can cook for dinner tonight. You get so wrapped up in the details that you forget your big-picture goals. This often happens to Motor Mouths; they have so much to say about so many details that they fail to achieve their macro-level purpose.

They waste people's time. This is the Motor Mouths' cardinal sin—and also what keeps them from exerting real influence in their organizations. Nobody in today's über-busy world has time to listen to a colleague talk until she figures out what she's trying to say. The Motor Mouth who wastes colleagues' time will discover that people do not respect him, tune him out, and delay responding to his calls and e-mails. He'll ultimately find he has trouble getting others to help him put his ideas into action.

How to Dial Back Too Much Verbal Presence

Becca was the president of a young, growing software company. She was preparing for a big presentation in which she'd be pitching a new app to the board, which included some of the company's key funders.

She knew her material. She'd been a leading programmer for years and as one of the company's rising stars, her peers applauded her leap to the president's role. They were confident she'd represent their exciting new idea and get board approval. But after her first rehearsal of the presentation, the CEO called me in a panic.

"I could barely understand a word she was saying, and I already know what the app is supposed to do!" he told me. "You've got to help her—we need the board's approval on this!"

The first time I sat through Becca's presentation, I didn't understand a word of it either. She spent most of the time talking about the technical aspects of how the app would work (I think). When she was finished, I still didn't know what the app was going to do.

Becca had a classic *Motor Mouth* problem. And she was usually very centered with her fellow programmers. She knew what information they'd need and she could share it succinctly—because her colleagues spoke her language. The problem was that she hadn't changed her style to present to a nontechie audience. She needed to translate her presentation into corporate-board-speak.

Becca and I went back to the drawing board. We started with the basics: what the app would do, who would download it, and why. I helped her come up with a story about the problems the app would solve for a typical user to help the board see the big-picture goal of this new project—and, most important, its financial viability.

Start with the big picture

We kept her talk short and light on technical details. This would leave the board with plenty of time to ask questions. It sounds paradoxical, but omitting the particulars from the body of her talk was the best way to present her idea to the board. This way, instead of drowning them in technical information that they didn't understand, Becca would *ground them in the big picture context* and then let them ask about whatever details they wanted to know. They'd end up remembering those details better because there'd be fewer of them, and they'd be grounded in context.

TIPS   *If you've got too much verbal presence, you can try some of these tips to stay centered:*

Choose the right difficulty level. Michel overwhelmed his board because he spoke at an introductory level to people who were ready for an advanced seminar, while Becca did the opposite. Think about your audience. How much do they already know? What will they want to hear, and what information will help you move them to the action you want them to take?

Aim for a light sprinkling of salt. Details are important, but don't overwhelm your audience with too much data. Try to give people *just enough* information. Your goal is to be like salt—to create a thirst for more.

Win the game in Q&A. It's always a bad sign when the audience sits stupefied at the end of a presentation. When you hit that sweet spot of giving people just enough detail, they'll be excited to engage with you and will ask better questions. You'll find you're having a *conversation* instead of just delivering an information dump—which will make the experience on both sides more satisfying.

Stop informing; start influencing. If all you need to do is give someone a few facts, you could just send them an e-mail. Think of communicating as a transfer of emotion, not information. Your goal with any important communication should be to *move someone to action*. Remember to start with your ideal outcome—the action you want to influence your audience to take—and work backwards from there.

Simplify to amplify. What you *leave out* is every bit as important as what you include. Think carefully about every data point or idea you might incorporate. Ask yourself: does this point advance my big-picture goal? If not, leave it out, and let your audience ask about it if they're curious. Remember, simplicity is a complex business. It's easy to simply open the fire hydrant and spew everything you know. It's much harder to craft a *focused* message.

Aim for a high signal-to-noise ratio. We're all drowning in information these days. Make sure that too many messages don't add to the problem. Don't let your idea get drowned out by noise—a confused listener is a passive listener.

Run your business, not your mouth. Don't just talk for the sake of talking. Make sure you have something to *say*. Keep thinking about your objectives, and make sure you're communicating to advance those objectives. Staying focused on your audience and your purpose will help you craft more effective messages.

Earn attention. Everyone's entitled to their opinion—but that doesn't mean anyone else has to pay attention to it. You don't deserve attention just because you show up. You *earn* it by being centered in verbal presence—by knowing what you have to say and saying it well.

Don't waste people's time. Keep in mind that everyone you're talking to is just as busy as you are. Your time is precious; so is theirs. They'll be happy to hear a crisp, focused message.

Don't get drunk on social media. Social media is dangerous for Motor Mouths, because it offers a constant temptation to overshare. Treat these sites just as you would any other form of communication: think about what your audience wants to know and deliver focused messages.

Use shorter sentences. It sounds silly, but it works. Your audience will get lost in a long, winding sentence, whether it's on paper or in person. Keep it simple. Keep it focused. Make important sentences pop by being shorter.

How to Manage a Motor Mouth

If you work with a Motor Mouth, don't just duck their calls or back away slowly when they approach the coffee machine. Remember, they're not just wasting your time; they're undermining their own effectiveness and yours, too. You'll be doing them a favor if you can find a way to help them stay focused. The fact that you'll be making your own work life better is an added bonus.

TIPS

Here are some tips for dealing with a colleague with excessive verbal presence:

Interrupt well. Michel's board learned the hard way that saying "OK, got it" doesn't always work with a Motor Mouth. It has to be specific. This will help The Motor Mouth feel that you've recognized his or her contribution. Instead try to say something like: "It sounds like you're saying . . ." and then sum up her point.

Pass the ball. If your colleague is dominating a conversation, firmly but politely make them give someone else the floor. Here's how: Sum up his point, then ask a direct question of someone else to move things along. It could be something like "Great contribution, Tim. Sarah, what's your point of view?" Physically move away from The Motor Mouth if you're standing.

Ask the right question. Remember Dean, the CEO from Chapter 6, on centered verbal presence? He listened to Tim's off-target pitch, and then he asked the one question that would get Tim focused on the big picture ("Where's the profit potential?"). When your colleague gets lost in the weeds, ask the right question that will help them refocus.

Set clear boundaries. If your colleague often talks too long in a casual context, tell him right away that you've got a full schedule and you only have a few minutes to chat. Then, if possible, set some time aside for lunch or coffee dates so he doesn't feel slighted.

Establish meeting rules. Meetings can tend to be a free-for-all in some office cultures. If enough people are upset, why not work out a system for taking turns? Allot a time limit and seek contributions from everyone. If people know they'll have an opportunity to talk, they'll be more likely to wait their turn.

Stand your ground. If your colleague interrupts you a lot, sometimes you must interrupt them in turn, with a polite retort. Try saying something like, "Excuse me, Debbie, but I didn't get to finish. I'd like to add that . . ."

Talk to them directly. If holding the floor doesn't stop the interruptions, privately inquire, "Did you realize that you frequently interrupt me? Is there something I can do to help solve the issue?" Often, people are accustomed to being rewarded for being a contributor and they have no idea that they're being rude or hurting your feelings.

Stay on target. Don't let your colleague distract you with irrelevant details. If you're centered and focused on your big-picture goals, you should be able to tell which points you need to discuss and which are merely distractions. When your colleague gets off track, steer the conversation back to the point.

Simplify to amplify

French philosopher Blaise Pascal once wrote, "I would have written a shorter letter, but I did not have the time." Focused communication isn't easy; but it's crucial in today's information-flooded world. Michel and Becca both learned to tailor their messages to their audiences—to cut out the noise and amplify the signal. If they can do it, so can you!

....

THE 10 WORST E-MAIL MISTAKES

Let's say you get 100 e-mails a day. (Everybody wants to "keep you in the loop.") Do you realize how much of your time this is eating up? If each e-mail takes up three minutes of your time, it takes you five hours to read and respond. *Five solid hours!* No wonder you're having trouble getting things done—you're stuck in e-mail jail.

Ready to tame this time-sucker? Let people know that starting today, you're adopting a new policy to help everyone lighten the load. You *can* gradually train others to stop overloading you with e-mails; but it starts with you. The better you *send*, the better you *receive*.

Here are the 10 worst e-mail mistakes and how to correct them before sending your next e-mail.

Are you guilty?

1. **Using e-mail as your automatic weapon.** Don't impulsively tap away just because e-mail is your favorite method. Pick up the phone or—*gasp*—actually talk to someone face-to-face. This can speed things up considerably. Also, don't assume that people have read what you sent them three hours ago. If you're sending time-sensitive or critical information, use the dual format: follow up your e-mail with a brief, heads-up confirmation call.

2. **Using wimpy or lazy subject lines.** Use the subject line to briefly summarize important content. Make it meaningful and timely to the

recipient because most of us *scan* the subject lines in order to decide whether we'll open, forward, or trash incoming messages. Don't leave the subject line blank or write wimpy, generic lines like "FYI," "The File You Requested," or "Project Update." Be more specific and informative. And don't be lazy and keep replying with the same subject line. Refresh your subject line as the subject changes.

3. **Burying the lead.** It's rude to force someone to wade through two screens of information before you get to the action that you're requesting. If you want to get things done, say so in the first paragraph. Frontload your e-mail with what matters most. Think *newspaper headline*. Lead with what's new and what you want the reader to absorb and act upon.

4. **Babbling text without bullets.** Because most people don't read past the first page, try to whittle your e-mail down to one screen or less. Plus, we often hit "reply" before we finish reading the whole thing, anyway. If you have several items to convey, create a list. *Number or bullet your points* so they jump off the screen and are easy for the reader's brain to process. Be as pithy as possible. Brevity leads to quicker, better responses.

5. **Habitual use of High Priority! flagging.** We all know the story of the boy who cried wolf, don't we? Overusing the *High Priority!* flag makes you that boy. Just because it's important to you does not make it important

to the recipient. The flag means that information is *time-sensitive* and needs *action straightaway*. It's not a status symbol or power play. Don't use it to convey "The boss's name is in here, so open it now!" or for messages like "We have a new employee!"

6. **Tone-deafness.** E-mail is a magnet for misunderstandings. Sometimes we send words that unintentionally rub others the wrong way, depending upon our—or their—current frame of mind. Gut-check your e-mails by asking: How would *I* interpret this if it landed in *my* in-box? Also, refrain from sending or responding to emotional e-mails in the workplace. Think of sending an e-mail as sending a postcard: If you wouldn't want it pinned to the bulletin board, don't send it.

7. **Copying too many people.** Routinely copying in lots of people is a heinous crime. Ask yourself: "Why am I sending this to *each recipient*?" Let people know at the start of the message specifically what they should *do* with it. Do they need to make a *decision*? Is *action* required? Or are you sending it so that they're *aware* of the information? If you're sending it just to cover your butt, don't send the copy. As for BCC (blind carbon copy), its purpose is to protect the e-mail addresses of certain individuals when sending bulk messages—not to send stealthly, sneaky copies. And "Reply All" is *usually* simply a mistake. Rarely do you need to reply to *everyone*—unless you enjoy grandstanding or being on a power trip.

8. **Grammar and misspellings.** As most of us know, reading from a screen is more difficult than reading from paper. Use standard capitalization and spelling. DON'T USE ALL CAPS—IT LOOKS LIKE YOU'RE SHOUTING! and don't use all lower case—it signals laziness. Make your e-mail personal by adding a greeting at the top. Skip lines between paragraphs. (White space is good.) And *always proofread*. If an e-mail is really important, consider *printing* a copy to proof it. You'll often catch mistakes on paper that you didn't notice on the screen.

9. **Forwarding without editing.** Don't just forward e-mails intact if the recipient didn't intend for their thoughts to be passed along. Do a little triage to make it appropriate for the recipient. Edit out any personal comments that could get the original sender in trouble.

10. **Sending unwanted attachments.** Your goal is to reduce the number of steps that your recipient must take in order to act upon your message, right? Then don't bog them down. When possible, copy and paste the most relevant passages into the body of the e-mail. Besides, you can bring down an entire e-mail system with a file that's too large or virus-laden—and some systems automatically remove attachments, anyway.

Finally, a bonus recommendation since you made it this far: Stop checking your e-mail obsessively. Turn off the "auto-check" feature that pings every few minutes, and limit yourself to checking e-mail at intervals throughout the day. You'll give yourself breathing room to focus and get things done again.

....

Verbal Presence Review

TOP 10 TIPS FOR CENTERING YOUR VERBAL PRESENCE

1. **Identify your ideal outcome.** Start with what you want your audience to do and craft a message that will take them there.

2. **Put it on paper.** Seeing something in writing lets you review your idea and fix it if necessary.

3. **Avoid crutch words.** Learn to pause when you're thinking of what to say next instead of stalling for time with filler words.

4. **Focus on your audience.** Think carefully about what your audience wants and needs to hear.

5. **Listen well.** Don't just wait for your turn to talk—learn to *want* to hear what your colleagues are saying.

6. **Think like an analyst.** Provide the context and connections that will engage your audience—don't simply throw information at them.

7. **Win the game in Q&A.** Give just enough detail to create a conversation, not an information dump.

8. **Enforce order.** Make sure your team doesn't drown out the quieter voices among its members.

9. **Don't get drunk on social media.** Treat these sites just as you would any other

form of communication—think about what your audience wants to know and deliver focused messages.

10. **Ask the right questions.** Help your colleagues stay focused on the big picture.

**Verbal
Presence
Action Plan**

Identify the top three conditions that knock your verbal presence off-center:

1. _____

   _____

2. _____

   _____

3. _____

   _____

Three ways you plan to keep yourself centered in verbal presence:

1. _____

   _____

2. _____

   _____

3. _____

   _____

LAYER THREE: OUTER PRESENCE

HOW OTHERS EXPERIENCE YOU

Transform the Way People Respond to You

9

What Is
Outer Presence?
Managing Your Reputation

Step through the front doors of any corporate
headquarters, anywhere around the globe, and
you'll hear the term *executive presence* being ban-
died about. Everybody wants it—but nobody
seems to know exactly what it means.

Most people associate executive presence with
external appearance—that is, what you *look* like.
Presence is conveyed by the dark-colored suits that
exude authority for men or the fashionable yet
classic clothing that projects success in women.
After spending more than a decade as an executive
coach—and, before that, two decades in television,
a medium where colleagues and viewers alike
ruthlessly judge appearances—I've certainly
learned that the way we look does matter. But
ultimately I believe that people have this executive
presence thing backwards. I've arrived at a completely different definition of outer presence:

**How you make
people feel**

147

Your outer presence is how you make people feel.

In nearly every encounter, every day—from when you get your morning coffee to whom you encounter on your commute home—people make snap judgments about you based on how you make them feel. Long before they judge the merit of your ideas, they *prejudge* you based on how you come across. And one of the ways they decide whether you're the real deal is to determine whether you're being "authentic." Here we go again, encountering yet another nebulous buzzword in the corporate world—*authenticity*. Let's consider what authenticity really means.

Authenticity is the courage to show up as yourself.

That means not adding a layer to your persona and trying to come across as someone who is better than who you already are. And it means not stripping off a layer with false humility, either. Authenticity means being *who you are*, no matter where you are, at what time of day, or who else is there.

The courage to show up as yourself

Trust is the major issue at stake here. When you have a centered outer presence and show up as yourself, people feel they can trust you. In return, they reward you with priority status—in much the same way you might get priority status with an airline. In that case, you get the perks of boarding first, getting the best overhead bin space, and so on. Back on the ground, centered presence has its own rewards. People return your phone calls first and answer your e-mails first. They allow you to influence their decisions and actions and say "yes" to your requests via shortcuts without exhausting back-and-forth discussions—all because they trust you.

On the other hand, when your outer presence is off-kilter, people are skeptical of you. They may even distrust you. You could have the greatest idea in the world, but if something about you doesn't feel right to them, they will reject the idea. And possibly reject you as well.

Have you experienced this with someone else? Perhaps you were ready to buy an appliance, but a salesman turned you off so much that you walked away and took your business elsewhere. Or maybe a vendor at the office had the best product, hands down; but the salesman's attitude was so offensive that you awarded your business to a competitor instead.

I asked the participants in my Presence Project research, which you first read about in the opening chapter, to judge their own outer presence. Specifically, I wanted to know: did they feel as though they were centered, projected too much, or displayed too little?

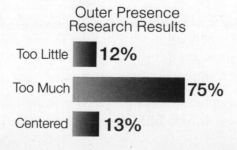

Outer Presence
Research Results

Too Little **12%**

Too Much **75%**

Centered **13%**

Most people think they're faking it

As you can see, a whopping 87 percent said their outer presence was off-center. So—where do you fall on this chart? How would *you* answer these questions?

Your outer presence is more relevant today than ever before because it has never been more prominent. You're now showing up *everywhere*. You may be on social sites like LinkedIn, Facebook, Twitter, and Instagram; opportunities to show your presence on social media are multiplying like rabbits. Not to mention your text messages, e-mails, and voicemails. People have so many new ways to experience you—and they're increasing every day.

We're all broadcasters now

If you think about it, all of us are now broadcasters—or at the very least, "narrow"-casters. You're disseminating information to a tribe of people. Your saturation rate is escalating. That's why your outer presence—*the way you make people feel*—has shifted into overdrive. And whether you participate in social media or not, your presence has never been more visible and more crucial to your success.

So—are you making the most of the opportunities that come your way? Or are you projecting *too little* outer presence, so that people don't even notice you in the room? Perhaps you do the opposite and come on too strong with *too much* outer presence, projecting a façade of power that people instinctively label as false.

Remember the word cloud method that we discussed in the Introduction? You identified an optimal word to define yourself at your best. Now it's time to pinpoint how *others* define you. The impression that others form of you is the ultimate outcome of your outer presence, so don't sugarcoat it. This is the time for brutal honesty.

Take a moment to write down the word that people use most often to describe you—even if it's not flattering.

How people describe me:_____
_____
_____.

How do others describe you?

If your outer presence is centered, you'll find that people describe you the same way you describe yourself at your best. If you're off-center, the two words won't match. And to make things more complicated, your outer presence changes from one interaction to the next. Most of us project an ever-shifting mix of honesty and artifice, depending upon the situation or people with whom we're dealing.

Why is this? It comes down to a simple but important concept: *intent* versus *impact*. You may *intend* to come across one way, but you may inadvertently *impact* others another way. If you're centered, your intent and impact are aligned. If you're off-center, they're uneven, which causes you to lose respect, trust, relationships—and maybe even your job.

A centered outer presence will allow you to influence the people around you more effectively, because your outer presence determines whether people are open to what you have to say. Think of it as your personal brand of leadership. Does it align with who you are? Or do you need to fine-tune it a bit?

Throughout this section, you'll see that outer presence is based on two fundamental, essential qualities:

1. **Likability.** Do people *like dealing* with you?
2. **Credibility.** Do they *respect* you?

These qualities are essential; they directly impact the decisions others make about you. The question is: Is your outer presence aligned with who you really are? Or, like most of us, could it use a little tweaking?

Let's explore this more in the following chapters.

10

Centered Outer Presence

"Why do you need me?" I asked Roger. Sitting in his gleaming corner office, I really *wasn't* sure why he had asked me to come in. Roger seemed like a calm and centered guy. He had just finished telling me that he thought he was pretty good at delivering speeches and dealing with the media, and based on his steady, empathetic demeanor, I believed him.

Transforming how others respond

"There's no endpoint when it comes to personal development," Roger said, leaning forward across his mahogany desk. "I need to keep learning every day. That's why I called you."

Roger was the new president of a Fortune 500 company. His predecessor had "retired" after a disastrous year in which the company missed its numbers—by double-digit millions. Customers were also frustrated with his predecessor because the organization missed delivery dates and had quality issues. Roger wanted customers to have a better experience and recommit to his company. Just as important, he wanted to create a new corporate culture of accountability, engagement, and candor for his tens of thousands of employees. If that wasn't enough, he also wanted to communicate clearly to his board of directors so they would understand how hard his team was working to turn the company around.

"We've got a lot of work to do," Roger said. "I want to make sure I set the right tone from the start."

Roger was a savvy guy. He knew how he'd feel if a new gun was brought in to lead his faltering team. "I'm sure they think I'm a hatchet man," he told me.

How do you make people *feel*?

Roger moved around a lot while growing up, and he had learned to be agile and intuitive. He understood that different people could hear the same message in different ways. He knew that in order to establish trust with his new employees, he needed to come across as both competent and approachable, and follow through on his promises.

He appeared comfortable, humble, and eager to hear his employees' ideas at the first all-hands meeting. He focused on the future rather than the past. "It's time to get on the right path now," he said. He told them he was excited about their potential to perform at a higher level and to reach their own personal development goals. Word spread that the new boss was *the real deal*.

Outer presence is about how you make people *feel*—and Roger wanted his staff to feel engaged, accountable, and empowered to make major changes to grow the business.

What Centered Looks Like

A balanced outer presence is an asset for any business leader. Steve Jobs's successor as CEO of Apple, Tim Cook, projects it. He even looks like an Apple product: understated, yet powerful. Nothing about his outer presence keeps his people from feeling valued and comfortable.

Cook inherited the world's most valuable corporation from a great showman, but he's made Apple his own. He hasn't tried to imitate Steve Jobs. He's earned respect by projecting competence in his own style, thereby earning people's trust. Unlike his predecessor, Cook is soft-spoken. He doesn't "come after" you in the manner that Jobs did; he *invites* you in. He developed his professional and people skills while he rose through the ranks at IBM and Compaq, before Jobs brought him in to lead operations at Apple.

When illness forced Jobs to speed up his organization's succession planning, he didn't want a knock-off as a replacement. He wanted *the real deal*. And so he chose Cook.

After his appointment in 2011, Cook told *Time* magazine, "I decided from negative time zero—a long time before [Jobs] talked to me about his decision to pass the CEO title—that I was going to be my own self. That's the only person that I could do a good job with being."

Cook appears to be at ease showing his true self to others and tapping into their feelings. And just as important, he openly apologizes when things go awry—like he did with the Apple Maps mess (when the company booted the beloved Google Maps app from the iPhone in favor of their own, inferior app) or the recent warranty issues in China. After China's Central Television accused the company of second-rate repair service in its country in March of 2013, Cook immediately posted an apology letter on the Chinese version of Apple's website. His letter ended:

> *We appreciate the feedback that we've received, and we have a tremendous respect for China. Our customers here will always be central to our thoughts.*
> *—Tim Cook, Apple CEO*

A centered leader respects others

That's what balanced outer presence looks like—a centered leader who values and respects others. Others feel it and respond positively.

One of Cook's former peers, Ron Johnson, was the Senior Vice President of Retail Operations at Apple. You've seen Johnson's hallmark design if you've ever visited an Apple Store. He pioneered the Apple retail experience—from the Genius Bar to the stores' entire look and feel. His strategy and implementation were, indeed, genius. After opening their retail locations, Apple experienced explosive growth, exceeding a billion dollars in sales within two years' time. Apple customers feel valued and cool when they enter the stores. I stop by Apple Stores in nearly every city I visit just to take in the energetic vibes—and countless other people do, too.

Johnson was lured away from Apple to become the new CEO of JC Penney in November 2011. And that's when things went terribly wrong in his career. Why? Because of how he made JC Penney customers *feel*. Almost as soon as he signed on, Johnson implemented a radical retail redesign and did away with—*gasp*—the coupons and sales upon which regular shoppers had come to rely. Customers felt alienated, which caused a disastrous drop in sales—25 percent during Johnson's first year. As a result, profitability plummeted. Insiders claim Johnson implemented these sweeping changes without first conducting customer research. The board ousted Johnson in April 2013. After all, board members have feelings too—and apparently they felt better reinstalling former CEO Don Ullman to win back customers' hearts and dollars.

Of course, the importance of being one's authentic self extends far beyond the boardroom—and even the business world. When Pope Francis was elected in early 2013, his early actions as the new head of the Catholic Church made people *feel* something had changed for the better. The former Cardinal Jorge Mario Bergoglio had long been known for living a simple life in his home country of Argentina; he cooked his own meals and took the bus just like everyone else. He even paid for his own hotel bill after the conclave in March 2013. At his inaugural mass, he dressed more simply than many of his predecessors, and stepped out of his official car to shake hands and bless a sick man in the crowd.

In his first homily, Pope Francis said, "Let us never forget that authentic power is service." His tone, demeanor, and style have so far reinforced that humble message. You don't have to be Roman Catholic to admire this appreciation for genuineness. People sense that Pope Francis is indeed "the real deal"—which assures them that they can trust his leadership.

Throughout much of her storied career, legendary performer Whitney Houston had a centered outer presence.

"She was both ordinary and extraordinary at the same time," the Reverend Al Sharpton told *Newsweek* after her death in 2012. "You saw her beauty, but you weren't overwhelmed by it because she wasn't arrogant. You heard her talent, but you weren't envious of it because she felt like a friend."

Houston had a balanced outer presence. She had the three degrees of energy (which you'll read about in a moment): facial, vocal, and body. And though she may have struggled internally, she made other people feel at ease using these three elements.

Three Degrees of Personal Warmth

These three degrees of energy combine to create personal warmth. Long before people consider the merit of your ideas, they prejudge you based on your warmth. It's the first thing that people assess about you. Whitney Houston oozed warmth—at least when she was in public.

How about you?

If people perceive your warmth, they're more likely to be open to your ideas and trust you—and if they trust you, they're more likely to follow your leadership. But as I've learned from a decade of coaching, your likeability factor *plummets* if people feel that you're lukewarm or cold toward them.

Let's stop here for a moment—because I believe most people have the notion of likability fundamentally backward. The problem is not that people don't like *you*. It's that they think *you* don't like *them*.

When you radiate warmth, people feel that you understand them and care about their well-being. And this matters because of the psychological principle of *reciprocity*.

At the most basic level, the first question our unconscious minds ask when we meet someone new is: friend or foe? We answer this question based on those three degrees of personal warmth: facial expression, tone of voice, and body language.

Forced smiles and genuine grins are two different things. Disingenuous smiles do more harm than good—and there are actually *two* types of smiles:

1. **Natural smiles.** When you do this, you contract the muscles around both your

1. FACIAL WARMTH
What does your face reveal?

mouth and your eyes. Your crow's feet—if you're old enough (like me) to have them—are engaged in this kind of smile. A natural smile is contagious and makes people feel that you're genuine.

2. **Fake smiles.** This version involves the mouth only and makes people feel that you're disingenuous or even a bit shifty. Fake smiles are often used at the wrong time, to mask inner feelings. Oddly enough, those with a lot of dental work may be perceived as flashing fake smiles even when they're genuinely happy, because dental work can make the lips move unnaturally.

A forced smile will register as insincere to the people around you. If you plaster on a grin when you walk into a meeting, you'll project too much outer presence. You'll come across as The Pretender. On the other hand, if you walk around looking bored—if you wear the "McKayla Maroney is not impressed" face or the "Grumpy Cat" face (both made famous online)—others will experience you as cold or disinterested, regardless of your intention.

What does your face look like? We all have a neutral expression—that is, the way our face looks when we're not thinking about much of anything. If friends or coworkers tend to tell you to "cheer up" or often ask you, "What's wrong?" your neutral expression is probably an unhappy one. But don't feel bad—most of ours actually are. And the older we get, the more our faces fall to the floor, sadly.

People are better at spotting a phony than you might think. Researchers at Wales's Bangor University found that people instinctively prefer to interact with someone who has a genuine smile over someone who's smiling only to be polite—and in order to prefer the real smiles, they had to be able to distinguish them from the fake ones. The lead researcher on the smile study, Erin Heerey, said that the key difference is in the laugh lines around the eyes. So let those crow's feet show! They make you more influential.

You exhibit the second degree of warmth through your *voice*.

2. VOCAL WARMTH
What voice do others hear?

Is it possible you don't realize how disinterested or bored you sound? That's because you hear a different version of your voice than anyone else does.

You have a skewed perception of your voice. Inside your head, your voice sounds bigger, brighter, and a lot nicer than it does when it leaves your body, mixes with oxygen, and others hear it. Why is that? It's like a shower stall inside your head. You have 80 muscles in your cranium, in addition to bone and brain matter, that resonate with the sound of your voice.

Of course, it's not only our speaking voices that affect other people. Researchers found that Grammy-winning singer-songwriter Adele's powerhouse voice elicits chills during ballads such as "Someone Like You." Singers who can achieve this kind of vocal dissonance provoke strong emotions that produce dopamine in your brain. *Psychology Today* explains that dopamine is a neurotransmitter that helps regulate movement and emotional responses. It enables us not only to feel and identify rewards, but also to *take action*. While we can't all be Adele, we *can* all learn to speak in a more resonant tone and vary our vocal pace and patterns to move people.

3. BODY WARMTH

Does it reinforce or reveal?

We reveal the third degree of warmth through our *body language*.

The importance of body language has been thoroughly discussed and documented over the past few decades. And while I agree that it's certainly crucial, I believe you project the best body language when you pair it with the other two degrees of warmth. Your body language should reinforce what your face and voice are projecting. Otherwise, you're just posturing.

Speaking of posture, I sat on a phone book during my time behind the anchor desk. Sound weird? Allow me to explain why.

I sat next to many male coanchors for 20 years of delivering the news on television. Some of these fellows were a foot taller than me. Men are also the ones who usually design and construct television news sets, with the desk height created to comfortably seat and showcase an anchorman's long torso. If I, at 5 feet 5 inches, planted my tush squarely on the chair beside my male coanchors, I would come off looking like their *little sister*.

So I decided to even the playing field—literally. I boosted my backside in order to have an equal "seat at the table." By sitting on a phone book, my outer presence appeared equal to my taller cohorts. (Of course, my coanchors would occasionally whip out their own phone books as a prank; but that's another story.)

People's perceptions of your presence can elevate or diminish your leadership. Individuals with a centered outer presence are conscious of how their physical presence makes other people feel. They therefore take action to create the best possible impression—even if a little outside help is required.

Traits of Centered Outer Presence

Bob was a vice president gunning for a spot on the executive team whose boss had told him that he didn't quite "fit in." But nobody wanted to tell Bob *specifically* what was holding him back.

Somehow they thought he'd guess that "fit in" really meant "get fit." But he didn't; so I got to break the news as part of my coaching assignment to help Bob gain executive presence and the board's approval.

Most people in the business world don't want to talk about appearance, likely fearing legal action—but it *does* matter. Bob was 50 pounds overweight, and it was interfering with his ability to move forward professionally. A recent study by the Center for Creative Leadership found that executives who are carrying extra pounds or have higher body-mass-index readings are considered less effective than their leaner peers. Physically fit CEOs were seen as more competent, and their peers also reported that they had better interpersonal skills.

Bob's outer presence was off-center in other ways, too, which is why his boss called me in. Senior executives told me Bob knew his stuff and was excellent at his job, but he cranked up the volume when challenged in meetings. He also failed to project authority and confidence when he walked into a room.

Appearance does matter

TIPS   *Here are some of the key characteristics of the centered outer presence that we all need to develop:*

Appear approachable. Why did so many people fall in love with actress Jennifer Lawrence the night she won her Best Actress Oscar for *Silver Linings Playbook*? Because she's so relatable—and because her nonverbal signals were completely in line with what she was saying. When she tripped and fell while walking up the stairs to accept her statue, it sealed her as the real deal. As the star-studded audience gave the actress a standing ovation, she made light of the moment, saying, "Thank you so much. This is nuts. You guys are only standing up because I fell and you feel bad. That was embarrassing." Her outer presence was centered and comfortable—even after she hit the floor. The audience felt like she was the girl next door.

Be congruent. Are you knocked off-center by a lack of synchronicity between what you say verbally and what you communicate nonverbally? People look for congruency. They believe what they see, not what they hear. Our unconscious minds are very good at assessing congruency because we're wired for it. A team of Italian scientists studying monkeys in the 1980s and

1990s identified neurons that fired in the brain when the monkeys picked up a piece of food—and then found the exact same neurons fired when the monkeys *watched another monkey* pick up a piece of food. Scientists say these neurons, now known as mirror neurons, exist in our brains as well. They're the reason we wince when we see someone else get hurt, for example. We understand what the people around us are doing because at some level *we're doing it with them*. That's why congruency matters. It helps us into other people's intentions.

Own Your Space

I was reminded of this crucial trait when I watched a U.S. presidential news conference in 2009 announcing the nominations of two women to high posts. President Obama spoke first to make the nominations, so the podium microphone was set for his height. Hillary Clinton, then-nominee for Secretary of State, spoke next. She had enough experience to move the double microphone down a few inches so it didn't hide her face in the press photos. Good move.

Next came then-nominee for United Nations ambassador Susan Rice. When Rice, a Rhodes Scholar and former Brookings Institution fellow, stepped to the microphone as the final nominee, *she sounded smart—but looked silly*. Her diminutive frame positioned her in a way that the microphone came all the way up to her eyeballs, totally obliterating her face.

Picture the scene in your mind: it was a double microphone. There were two black spheres and both were hiding Rice's eyeballs. As Rice's head bobbed up and down reading her notes, the hardware danced from her eyeballs to her forehead. It was almost comical—and it made it hard to concentrate on a word she said. Let that be a lesson for all of us: adjust your microphone in order to safeguard your dignity. Rice needed to take ownership of her space in order to ensure her outer presence kept people focused on her intellect and ideas, and not be distracted by a silly scene.

Look the part   You may believe that things like your weight or the way you dress are superficial, and that your colleagues should judge you solely on your performance. Believe me, I sympathize. But those seemingly superficial elements are anything but superficial in the business world.

First of all, you need to ensure your appearance doesn't distract people from measuring your *credibility*.

According to Walter Isaacson's book *Steve Jobs*, Jobs wanted his fellow employees at Apple headquarters in Cupertino, California, to wear uniforms so everyone would be on an equal playing field. He commissioned fashion designer Issey Miyake to design a company vest. But his employees balked at the idea. So he created a "uniform" for himself: black mock turtleneck, Levi's 501 jeans, and grey New Balance sneakers. "That's what I wear," Jobs told Isaacson as he opened his closet to reveal stacks of identical clothes. I'm not suggesting you wear the same outfit day in and day out—far from it—but I *do* embrace the idea of using your attire to send a consistent message.

Men do have it easier in this area. If you're a male in the corporate world, perhaps you wear a suit and tie every day. Grey, black, navy, brown; when you're feeling particularly hot to trot, maybe you go for pinstripes. Maybe take the jacket and tie off for casual Fridays.

Many women find it harder to strike the right balance with our clothing. We have so many choices in terms of hemlines, necklines, shapes, patterns, and colors (not to mention what we do with our makeup, hair, and accessories). But ultimately, every leader's goal is the same: look polished. Look appropriate. Don't let the way you package yourself on the outside diminish how people feel about you.

Because your outer presence is about how you make people feel, keeping centered requires paying attention to your face, voice, and body. It takes some time to master these skills; so don't panic if these tips sound overwhelming at first. You can work on them one at a time, and practice each until you feel comfortable.

Here are some strategies for staying centered: **TIPS**

Master the "Magic Move®." This simple trick will help you produce a warm, genuine smile no matter what the circumstances. Once you master it, people will see you as engaged and approachable. It works equally well to tone down a fake grin or to warm up a bored-looking neutral face. See the end-of-chapter feature for more on how to make this magic happen.

Stick out your gut. When you speak, push out your gut (yes, your gut), breathe deeply from your diaphragm, and unleash your full vocal range, not just the top register. Many people essentially choke themselves when they speak, because they talk only from the throat. Others talk from their heads, providing an irritating nasal sound. Go deeper.

Vary your pace. Sameness is the death of any speaker. You'll lull your listeners to sleep if you speak at the same steady pace all the time. A variable speed signals that *you're* excited and engaged—and when you're engaged, others are, too.

Don't sound scripted. Sounding contrived like this undermines your warmth and makes you come across as mechanical instead of *real*. That's why reading from text-laden slides makes people feel that you don't know what you're doing.

Don't speak too vehemently. It rubs people the wrong way if you're louder than the situation calls for. It says that you're judgmental and are trying to overpower others to get your way.

Don't speak too softly. On the other hand, you can diminish your outer presence if you don't speak loud enough, or if your voice quivers or squeaks because you're nervous. Some people's voices trail off at the end of sentences because secretly, they don't want to be heard. (I used to do that.) It might also happen because they're not breathing deeply enough to give them the breath support to finish the sentence strong.

Don't diminish yourself by hunching over. We're all falling prey to bad posture nowadays, brought on too many hours crouching over a computer screen. I call it "tech neck." Do you find yourself leaning forward a lot? Is your head craning forward? I've found that I have to reteach myself how to sit and stand up straight; you may need to, as well.

Calm your body. We're all rushing around non-stop today. Try to keep your movements smooth, calm, and deliberate so you appear comfortable and in control. Quiet your lower body especially; bouncing legs and happy feet are distracting.

Be aware of anxious consumption. And I'm not just talking about alcohol here; I mean *any* liquid. Senator Marco Rubio chugged a tiny bottle of water during his 2013 State of the Union Republican response, and took a distracting break during his live speech to do so. Rubio instantly became a punch line. In a swig heard 'round the world, he demonstrated why every executive must learn how to stay centered in outer presence.

Don't let your appearance distract from your message. I learned how easy it is for your audience to lose track of what you're saying in my years behind the anchor desk. I used to get letters from viewers, complaining that I'd worn the same color in a broadcast that I'd worn the week before. Mind you, it wasn't the same outfit, just the same *color*. But it was similar enough to distract my audience. I had to come up with a system that would keep me from repeating colors, since I'd discovered that it took some people's minds off my message. (You may be thinking, "Get a life!" about those viewers right now.)

Don't give people anything to focus their wandering minds on. Dangling earrings, jangling bracelets, and novelty ties can all potentially undercut your message. And yes—this is unfortunately harder for females. I've worked with a lot of women who didn't realize that their high hemlines or low necklines detracted from their executive presence and sent a message that they were a flirt, not a frontrunner.

Focus where your audience focuses

If you want to improve the way others experience you, *pay attention to what* they *pay attention to*. As I first wrote in *Talk Less, Say More*, people are engaged by what they want and value. This is how they connect to you. In order to strengthen your leadership, ask yourself whether you're tapping into what people specifically want and value.

You really do have to give this some careful consideration. In my coaching practice, I've seen many leaders delude themselves into thinking they know what people want. They *assume* they know—and unfortunately, they're often wrong. The solution is simple but profound: listen and watch carefully for what your target audience wants and values. Watch for the moments when they get emotional. Notice what topics they return to again and again. The answers are often hidden in plain sight.

Ron Johnson, JC Penney's newly ousted CEO, missed this step toward a successful outer presence. Yes, JC Penney needed a change when they hired him. But dismissing the feelings of the customers he was trying to influence was a fatal mistake.

My client Roger, on the other hand, instinctively understood how outer presence works—and he clearly demonstrated it when he spoke at the first all-hands meeting. His voice, face, and body language all communicated genuine warmth and openness.

As a result, his staff quickly committed to his proposed changes. They experienced him as approachable and trustworthy. And they've rewarded him with their trust and loyalty.

....

MASTER THE MAGIC MOVE®

Have you been to Paris? Like most tourists, when my daughter and I visited the magical city, the Louvre topped our "must-see" list. And what does every tourist want to see at the Louvre?

The Mona Lisa, of course.

And there she was, right in front of us—the most visited, most photographed, and most parodied painting in the world.

Everyone clamored around the display. As you can imagine, we were packed tighter than sardines to see Leonardo da Vinci's creation. The first thing you hear from people is "It's a lot smaller than I thought it would be."

Ambiguous. Enigmatic. Difficult to read.

Once you get past that marvel, you ponder another: the expression on her face. It's ambiguous. Enigmatic. Difficult to read. If you were to separate the Mona Lisa's face horizontally at the nose, you'd see two different emotions. Her mouth is easy to interpret: it's warm with a hint of a genuine smile. But the eyes. Oh, the eyes. They *are* mysterious.

That's why the painting is an enigma. Da Vinci didn't paint the full *Magic Move*. Allow me to explain: as you read earlier, the Magic Move is a technique I discovered in broadcasting that has the effect of warming up *anyone's* face. It makes you come across as pleasant, but not goofy. It solves the issues of looking grumpy or angry—which, as I also stated earlier, is how most of us inadvertently appear with our natural, neutral resting face.

Ready to try it? Place your index fingers at the corners of your mouth, and lift them up. Feeling silly yet? Now take your fingers away. You've just activated two of the 80 muscles in your cranium. Those two muscles are called your *levator labiis*, a broad sheet of muscles that connects your mouth to your eyes.

Look at yourself in the mirror now. Do you see how you've got just a hint of a smile on your face? How your eyes have developed a hint of a sparkle? You've just warmed up your face. Magical, isn't it?

It's a miracle cure for *The Ghost* or *The Pretender* —whom you will meet in the next chapter.

....

11

Too Little
The Ghost

"I look bored!" Kelly said. I'd just showed her footage of herself in a rehearsal interview we'd taped, and she was dismayed to realize that she wasn't coming across the way she intended. Instead of looking excited about the big opportunity that lay ahead of her, she looked downright unfriendly and disinterested.

Kelly and I were preparing for her big break. Her artwork was beginning to attract a lot of attention and would soon be featured at a major worldwide event. She'd have the chance to be interviewed by journalists from around the globe, and an opportunity to spark further interest in her work—*if* she could learn how to balance her outer presence.

Invisible at the wrong time

Kelly expressed herself powerfully in her art. Unfortunately, in person, she was invisible.

If we couldn't warm up her outer presence, Kelly risked having her interviews left on the cutting-room floor. She'd be cast aside at the very event that *should* have been the time and place for others to get to know who she truly was.

Everyone would see her work, but nobody would see *her*.

What Too Little Looks Like

Facebook CEO Mark Zuckerberg had an outer presence issue, too. He had a series of meetings with Wall Street analysts in May 2012, prior to his company's initial public offering. He wanted to garner $5 to $10 billion from the land of pinstripes and button downs. And he showed up wearing sneakers and a hoodie—a *hoodie*.

We can argue about whether it was a joke or a culture clash—but whatever he intended, the 27-year-old Zuckerberg conveyed a message to the analysts that he didn't respect them enough to dress appropriately for the occasion.

Wall Street analyst Michael Pachter told Bloomberg TV that day, "He's actually showing investors he doesn't care that much. I think it's a [sign] of immaturity. I think he has to realize he's bringing investors in as a new constituency right now, and I think he's got to show them the respect that they deserve because he's asking them for their money."

Like all presence issues, outer presence is *situational*. You may come across as confident in some situations and fade into the background in others.

I wrote in *Talk Less, Say More* about an early client I worked with, Don, who was a director in his company. His staff saw him as confident—even bossy—but when he was invited to executive team meetings, he didn't contribute. He was quiet as a church mouse.

His troubled CEO asked me to figure out if Don didn't know *how* to make a contribution, or if he just didn't *have anything to* contribute. His job was on the line.

Turns out, Don lacked executive presence in the *presence of executives*. He was a perfectionist, afraid to say the wrong thing in front of this powerful team. So he chose to stay mute in their presence. He thought it would reduce his risk of sounding as though he didn't know what he was talking about. But instead, it just made him seem like he had nothing to contribute.

Together, we designed a two-step plan to align Don's outer presence in these stressful situations. First, he'd play wingman. When someone else made a comment that he agreed with, he'd repeat the statement and add a few words. The executives responded well to this approach. Then he moved on to the second step: "planned spontaneity." I coached Don to study the meeting agenda in advance to figure out where he could make a meaningful contribution. We made sure that he made at least one contribution per meeting. Since he'd studied it in advance, he sounded confident and as though he were speaking off-the-cuff when he delivered his point.

Use "planned spontaneity"

Six months later, Don called me with big news. He'd been promoted and was now a vice president. He moved from *The Ghost* to the leadership team.

What knocks you off-center?

What circumstances make you collapse into yourself? When do you turn into The Ghost? Think of three times in the past year when your outer presence showed up as less than the real you. Write a brief description of each incident here:

1. _____

2. _____

3. _____

What do those three incidents have in common? Are you like Don, intimidated by people in power? Do you know what knocks you off-center and causes you to show up as less than yourself?

> *"George Bush doesn't care about black people."*
>
> —Kanye West

Are You Consistent?

Remember that moment? Kanye West's controversial statement at the 2005 Concert for Hurricane Relief came out of his personal experiences and political beliefs. But President George W. Bush had inadvertently left himself open to the criticism in the aftermath of Hurricane Katrina. The culprit? Outer presence.

In his comments following the storm, Bush delivered the traditional message, promising that the government would "do all we can to help people get back on their feet." But a photograph of him sitting and surveying the flooded region from the comfort of Air Force One undermined that statement. His words were *inconsistent* with his actions—and people believe what they see, not what they hear.

Contrast that visual with the indelible positive image of President Bush standing with emergency workers at Ground Zero three days after the September 11 attacks. When he grasped the bullhorn and declared, "I can hear you. The rest of the world hears you. And the people who knocked these buildings down will hear from all of us soon," his physical presence, strong stance, visible emotion, and the way he reached out to touch and connect with the people around him all underscored his powerful words. His words and actions were *consistent*.

As leaders, we all have to be vigilant about our outer presence—how we make people feel. It's situational. One day you may be a hero, and the next day you're the goat.

Are your words and actions congruent?

Projecting the right presence is particularly difficult in times of high emotion. When a fire crippled the *Triumph* and stranded passengers at sea for days in filthy conditions in February 2013, Carnival Cruise CEO (and Miami Heat owner) Micky Arison was harshly criticized for attending a basketball game during the crisis. It doesn't matter how worried he was about the situation; it wouldn't even have mattered if he'd spent the entire game on his BlackBerry, communicating with his staff. At a time when customers and the general public were (rightfully) upset with his company, he needed to be working harder than ever to show his customers that he cared about them.

To avoid sending the wrong message, think carefully about whether what you're doing feels right. Then think about how other people would feel about your actions.

When Penn State football coach Joe Paterno learned of his assistant coach Jerry Sandusky's crimes, he reported them to the college's athletic director and head of campus police—but not to the state police. Investigations concluded that he should have done more. At a moment when he should have taken decisive action as a leader, Paterno—who had before been a larger-than-life figure, a legend in the college football world— became a ghost. And that failure to act is now part of his legacy.

Hopefully, most of us won't be called on to report illegal actions in our working lives. But Paterno's example is still an important one. All of our actions—and just as important, our moments of *in*action—determine others' impressions of us.

If you disagree with an idea in a meeting, speak up respectfully, on the spot. Don't wait and send an e-mail later. If you have information that might affect a decision that's on the table, share it. It's your responsibility to contribute to your team. When you silence yourself, you rob others of ideas—and you become a ghost.

As these examples demonstrate, failing to project enough outer presence in a situation can turn you into The Ghost. Here are some of the most common ways this tendency manifests itself:

They physically make themselves smaller. Maybe you're like Kelly and you tend to slump instead of standing up straight. Or maybe you don't take the time to make the space your own when you enter a room for a presentation or meeting. Maybe you sink back in your seat, or fidget, or bounce your legs, or pace restlessly. You can train yourself out of these habits—the first step is to become aware of your body movements.

Their face appears disinterested. The next time you're waiting in line at a retail store, look around at the bored associates. How do they make you feel? Remember, you'll turn people off if your neutral expression looks bored or hostile.

Their voice sounds angry. If you're a ghost, you may have a tendency to speak too quietly, or pitch your voice too high to project confidence. Your sentences may trail off at the end as you secretly attempt to not be fully heard. You may even unconsciously add a question mark to the end of your sentences, making yourself sound unsure or in need of reassurance.

They're not visible. Yahoo! CEO Marissa Mayer was widely criticized for her 2013 decision to bring work-from-home employees back to the office. However, in her attempt to turn around the business, generate collaboration, and change the culture, she recognized that some of her 12,000

Traits of the Ghost

employees were becoming ghosts. While many initially grumbled for being called back to headquarters, Mayer may have done those remote workers a favor in the long run.

Many corporations are redesigning their headquarters to allow for more presence. Walls are tumbling down everywhere. Once-ubiquitous cubicles are being banished as workers no longer need to be tethered to their desks. Tech-savvy employees embrace the idea of collaborating from different open spaces in redesigned workplaces.

There's a whole new industry in favor of open spaces where people can gather and collaborate. Researchers at Carnegie Mellon University and Bosch Corporate Research found in 2008 that groups of software programmers who weren't physically together communicated less—and took 32 percent longer to finish their code. And a 2010 study of call-center employees by MIT researchers found that workers with strong social groups were more productive.

The title of that MIT study—"Productivity through Coffee Breaks"—hints at why *physically showing up* enhances not only your team's performance, but your own credibility. Think about your e-mail inbox. If you're like most modern workers, it's probably a source of constant stress. You're drowning in a flood of messages that all demand your attention. You get through them as quickly as you can. But when you're physically present at the office—when you step away from your desk for a moment and talk to your colleagues face to face—you hear more about what your colleagues are thinking and doing, and this can spark a new ideas for you.

If you're not projecting enough outer presence, you're undermining your own effectiveness.

Here are some ways to boost your outer presence:

See and be seen. For a worker who simply wants to put in the hours and stay in the background, there's nothing wrong with working remotely. But if you want to move up the corporate ladder, you must remember that visibility leads to credibility. Isolating yourself from your colleagues can undermine your credibility.

Choose to project power. Yes, you have to stand up straight. And when you walk into a room, you have to believe that you belong there. Move the chair, adjust the microphone. Take that seat in the center of the room. Do whatever you have to do to make the space your own.

Find your voice. Make sure you speak up enough that others can hear you. Breathe from your gut. Record yourself speaking and play it back; your voice is probably higher and less resonant than it sounds in your head, which undermines your authority. Practice until you find a tone that resonates.

Master the Magic Move. Do you remember how this move goes? You put your index fingers at the corner of your mouth and lift them up, making your face look warm and engaged. Practice in front of a mirror until it feels natural. Then, when you

How to Increase Low Outer Presence

TIPS

catch yourself looking bored or angry, pull those muscles up. Get used to making the Magic Move so that you don't have to think about it when you have an opportunity to influence and change minds.

Contribute. Speak up and share your ideas. If you're nervous around certain people in your organization, do what Don did: start out as a wingman. Chime in to clarify or support someone else's point. Then, once you become more comfortable speaking out, start raising new ideas.

Listen on purpose. Making your presence felt doesn't have to mean making the conversation all about you. Try an empathic listening technique: after a colleague speaks, say, "It sounds like you're saying . . ." and summarize their point. You'll help clarify the conversation—and you'll make yourself more visible.

Be willing to disagree. If you're nervous about speaking up at all, it will be even more difficult to do so when you disagree with a colleague. But it's a crucial skill to master. You can't be a wingman forever! Respectfully offering a different viewpoint is a bold way to make your mark in a conversation.

Assess before jumping in. Before you enter an unfamiliar situation—meeting with a new client, presenting at a conference, talking to higher-up executives—think carefully about what kind of outer presence you want to project. Will your normal style of dress be appropriate, or do you need to step it up, sartorially speaking? Should you contribute more or less than you typically would?

Give people what they value. What do they need to see and hear from you? Don't make the mistake of appearing indifferent, even callous, as President Bush did after Hurricane Katrina, or Micky Arison did during the cruise ship fiasco. Your audience can't read your mind, so they don't know what your intentions are. They only know what they see and hear. Give them what they need and value.

How to Manage a Ghost

If a colleague or friend is the one who's fading into the background, talk to them about it. They probably don't realize how invisible they've become. Maybe they don't know how dour their face looks. Slouching could be a habit they've been developing for years. Talking softly—or not contributing at all—may be their default status and they may not understand how it's holding them back.

TIPS

Here are some tips to help a Ghost make his or her presence felt:

Be direct, but compassionate. In order to help this person, you may need to expose a weakness they're not aware of. Deliver the news kindly but directly, so you don't embarrass or blame them. Think of how you'd tell them they had spinach in their teeth; it's precisely because you *don't* want them to be embarrassed that you're bringing it up.

Hold up a mirror. Offer to videotape them giving a presentation or doing a practice interview. They can't fix their flaws until they can face them.

Telling them they look angry or bored won't be as effective as *showing* them and letting them experience themselves as others do.

Be their wingman. If a colleague has trouble speaking up in meetings, it's important for their early attempts to go well. Give them positive reinforcement when they do contribute, and they'll be more likely to continue making contributions. Don't be disingenuous or condescending, but *do* thank them for raising valuable ideas.

Call out interruptions. Make sure the louder members of your team aren't talking over your Ghost. When you notice someone interrupting a colleague, call it out. Say, "I'm sorry, but I want to make sure I understand what Jamie is saying before we move on." Hopefully, a few interventions will teach your team to give each other enough space to speak.

Share how others see them. If inconsistency has undermined your colleague's message, let them know. Do it diplomatically—but do it. Don't let someone be the unknowing subject of gossip. Say, "I know you have a lot on your plate, but people misinterpreted it when you checked your e-mail during that meeting. It made them feel like you didn't care about Ellen's report."

Works Like a Charm   I taught Kelly, the artist, the Magic Move. It warmed up her face, making her look approachable and engaged. When Kelly mastered this move, it completely changed her outer presence. It unleashed her ability to look warmer, happier, and more excited about her work in our practice interviews. She stopped fading into the background, and started to stand out.

Later, she texted me from the big event: "Twenty-five interviews so far!!" I was thrilled to hear she was making the connections that could help her achieve mainstream success. She ended up on television and in newspapers around the world.

Kelly mastered the Magic Move and drew others in. She spoke from her heart and talked about her inspiration. The media and their viewers and readers experienced her as the warm, excited, talented artist that she was.

Her art made a giant splash—and so did she.

....

INFLUENCING YOUR TEAM'S CULTURE

Your leadership presence shapes the way your team behaves. If they see you as likable and credible, they'll feel comfortable being open and honest. Your style cascades throughout your entire team. Here are five ways to influence your culture:

Your presence shapes their behavior

1. **Set the tone.** An open, genuine presence based on your values is your best asset. A sense of self-preservation kicks in when team members fear your reactions. This defensive attitude leads them to withhold information. Nothing reinforces behaviors more than rewards. Integrate your values into your HR

process so that you measure and reward positive actions.

2. **Balance participation.** Some of your team members will try to dominate meetings, rendering others silent. Once this imbalance of participation is in place, it's hard to reverse. Watch for nonverbal signs that silent members want to contribute. Intervene if a few individuals do the lion's share of the talking, preventing the overall group from hearing differing points of view. Balanced participation will help you make the best leadership decisions possible.

3. **Squash suppression.** Suppressed disagreement is deadly. The last thing you want is for team members to censor strong negative feelings, since these feelings nearly always resurface as defensiveness and irrational criticism against you or other team members. Your role is to get hidden viewpoints on the table before they morph into damaging private agendas.

4. **Prevent groupthink.** A complete lack of conflict when discussing important decisions can be just as dangerous as suppression. It may signal that people are afraid to confront each other in an effort to preserve harmony. Groupthink often occurs in teams with minimal turnover. To counteract it, encourage rigorous discussions. Model, invite, and reward the candor you seek from your team members.

5. **Manage mistrust.** A culture of mistrust will derail your leadership. In the absence of trust, people question and resist even the most

innocuous suggestions. Delivering a clear and compelling agenda with transparency shapes a trusting culture. And it starts with your balanced outer presence.

....

12

Too Much
The Pretender

Antonio was anything but invisible. When he walked into a room, his aura almost bowled people over. He was super-smart, and he definitely wasn't shy about letting you know it. In fact, he told me during our first coaching session that his personal motto was, "I have a beautiful mind."

His aura bowled people over

Antonio was an aggressive, ambitious senior vice president—but his ambition had recently taken a hit. He should have been a leading candidate to succeed his global company's CEO, who planned to retire in a few years—but instead he'd just been passed over for a promotion to president that would have put him in line for the coveted corner office with the seven-figure annual salary.

Antonio was miffed about being overlooked. He didn't understand why he hadn't gotten the job, especially since he considered himself to be more qualified than anyone else for the position.

I, on the other hand, understood the reason for this perfectly—thanks to his latest 360-degree performance review. And I had to find a way to convey this to Antonio.

"Let's talk about your personal brand," I said to him in our first meeting. "How would you define yourself?"

"I'm direct," he said proudly.

"OK," I said, "let's take a look at your review and see if that's how your colleagues define you."

It wasn't. Instead of *direct*, they described him as *cutting*.

"Let's try again," I said. "What else would you say about yourself?"

"I'm agile," Antonio replied. "I understand complex ideas and implement them immediately."

Can you guess where this is going? Instead of *agile*, Antonio's colleagues saw him as *impulsive*. People had trouble following him because he seemed to change direction on a dime.

Antonio was projecting *too much* outer presence. His tough, forceful attitude overwhelmed people.

He was trying so hard to come across as a strong, quick-thinking leader that he unwittingly undermined his leadership power.

He was *The Pretender*.

What Too Much Looks Like

Early in news anchor Megyn Kelly's tenure at Fox News, network chairman Roger Ailes called her into his office. He told her he loved her look and her confidence—and then he said, "Now who's the *real you*?"

"It was like he was using x-ray vision to peer into my soul," Kelly told *Newsweek* in 2012. She realized that she was still holding onto pain from seventh grade when other girls had bullied her. Ever since then, she'd tried to appear bulletproof. She honed that aggressive attitude as a lawyer. But as a television anchor, her too-tough, too-perfect outer presence made it hard for some audience members to connect with her.

Until Ailes called her out.

He advised her to not be afraid to be vulnerable, and she took it to heart. Kelly told *Newsweek* it even changed the way she behaved around the man she later married. "Showing yourself," she said, "is risky; people might not like you. But it boosts the chances that other people can relate to you."

The Pretender comes across as false—but what's behind the façade? Here are some of the key characteristics that define people who have too much outer presence:

Traits of the Pretender

They're often insecure. This was the source of Megyn Kelly's excessive outer presence. Like her, many Pretenders feel unworthy, so they try to puff themselves up to appear bigger on the outside than they feel on the inside. Others, like Antonio, are just convinced they're the smartest person in the room. And maybe they are—but they're pushing so hard to make other people see it that they appear arrogant.

They appear over-rehearsed. Your energy level can reveal the truth behind a façade. You've probably seen overcoached politicians making stiff, wooden-arm gestures in debates or speeches; the vertical chop to emphasize a point is a perennial favorite. Audiences can tell that the politician is making those gestures deliberately.

Their voices drip with charm. A phony tone of voice can also damage how people feel about you. If you've seen the *Harry Potter* films, think of Dolores Umbridge. The character's sticky-sweet voice masks a heart of power-hungry evil, but that sweet voice doesn't fool you for a second, does it? If you're a *Simpsons* fan, think of Troy McClure, the host of every infomercial ever shown in Springfield. The second you hear the words, "Hi, I'm Troy McClure," you know you're in for some faked enthusiasm.

They're too loud or too enthusiastic. Failing to calibrate your enthusiasm to the occasion can also undermine your message. Remember Tom Cruise jumping on Oprah's couch? Maybe he really *was* over the moon about Katie Holmes.

But his manic excitement was so inappropriate for an interview that he came across as certifiably insane. I don't remember what movie he was promoting—only that he hopped up and down on that butter-yellow couch. Just one month after the couch incident, Cruise again demonstrated how important it is to match your energy level to the situation. Talking to Matt Lauer on the *Today* show about psychiatric prescriptions, he came across as a bully because he spoke forcefully and aggressively, even insulting women with postpartum depression like actress Brooke Shields.

As leaders, we all need to be aware of how others feel our presence. The higher up you move in an organization, the easier it is for you to become disconnected from the people you lead. Ground your message in your own experience, but don't presume to speak for anyone else.

Leaders must be aware of their presence

Pizza chain Papa John's CEO John Schnatter got into some PR trouble when he claimed that the Affordable Care Act, popularly known as Obamacare, would force him to either cut his employees' hours or raise prices. A survey by YouGov BrandIndex, which tracks the public perception of brands, found that the company's image took a significant hit from his comments.

Schnatter's wealth sets him very far apart from the low-wage workers whose hours he was threatening to cut. While I don't know his intentions, he may have wanted to come across as a business leader explaining the effect of proposed legislation. But because of his wealth and power, others experienced his statement as a threat: *do what I want or I'll pay you less and charge you more for pizza.*

How to Dial Back Too Much Outer Presence

Recently I was present at a leadership team retreat in South America. The executive team had brought in their young sales guns for a day. In a sales force filled with rising stars, it appeared that Jordan was the brightest. He had it all. Intelligence. Warmth. He even looked the part of the future company president.

While the executives were on a power walk in the woods that morning, I stayed behind to help the young guns rehearse the personal pitches they'd deliver to the executives that afternoon. Jordan practiced his first. If you'd read a transcript of his talk, it would have looked perfect. The same was true for his slides; they appeared flawless. But when he delivered his talk to his colleagues, Jordan added a layer to his personality—and he came across as too rehearsed. His colleagues tore him apart in their evaluations. They deemed his performance "affected" and "slick." He appeared to be putting on a performance—and it wasn't one that other people liked.

Preparation is crucial if you want to project a solid outer presence—but *overpreparation* can play havoc with your presence, too.

I played the videotape of Jordan's rehearsal for him. Seeing himself as others did smacked him right between the eyes. He was stunned that he came across as so slick. He was The Pretender.

I invited Jordan to come back to the front of the room and asked him a simple question, "Tell me what you love about sales. Just speak from your heart."

The change from "rehearsed Jordan" into "spontaneous Jordan" was powerful. His colleagues called it an amazing transformation. When he gave his talk again, this time to the executives in the afternoon session, it was incredible—because it was *real*. Just as real as the mud sticking to the executives' shoes after their morning power walk. They instantly loved him.

Jordan needed permission to be himself instead of pretending to be something more. Are you doing the same thing? Do you need to show your colleagues your humanity?

In the little frontier towns in Laura Ingalls Wilder's books, shopkeepers would put up false fronts—two-story facades that hid the one-story reality. The false fronts gave business owners more space to advertise and hinted at the promise of bigger and better things to come. They were common enough that people didn't feel tricked when they walked into the dingy little store behind the shiny facade. But when you put up a façade, it undermines your message. It makes it hard for people to relate to you or trust you, like Jordan.

Here are some ways to bring down your false front:　　**TIPS**

Tone down your grin. The Magic Move is great for people who look less engaged than they truly are, but it works equally well for those who come across as too phony or disingenuous, as well. Try practicing it. You'll appear warm and interested without coming on too strong or looking too slick.

Crank down the volume. Match your voice's tone and volume to that of the people around you. If your colleagues are chatting casually, don't let yourself overwhelm them. Even a slight volume difference can make people feel like you're over-powering them. This may take some work on your inner presence; if you're defensive, you're more likely to bellow and bluster in response to a simple question.

Consider their reality. If you have a big idea to present, first consider how your audience might experience what you're saying. Is there anything that might create a rift between what you're saying and how they're experiencing it?

Let people see your vulnerability. It may be difficult to let your guard down—especially in a competitive environment. But people won't trust you unless you show that you're willing to trust them, too. If you're tired, if your child is sick, if you have something going on—just admit it. Don't dwell on your problems, but don't try to hide your vulnerabilities, either. You're human—and as Megyn Kelly discovered, people experience you in a more positive way when you let them in.

Admit when you're wrong. Nobody's perfect. Don't be defensive, and don't make excuses: these give the impression that you're passing the buck. If something goes wrong, it's best to take respon-sibility for your mistakes.

If a colleague is coming across with a false front, you'll help them and improve your own working life if you can get them to tone it down.

Here's how to help a pretender:

Take the first step. An overly competitive atmosphere may encourage people to puff themselves up like peacocks. Showing that you're vulnerable may help your colleague calm things down. As a leader, show that you're open to and okay with hearing bad news, and be frank about your own limitations. As a member of a team, accept feedback graciously. It will encourage The Pretender to do the same.

Provide pragmatic feedback. Be candid when you're asked for feedback on a Pretender. Ask them if they want it straight. If so, let them know they tend to overpower a room. Gently explain how they're coming across. Imagine how helpful it would have been if someone on Antonio's team had spoken up and told him that they were confused by the way he kept changing his mind. He might have ended up securing the promotion he so ardently desired.

Share the love. If your colleague tries to hog the spotlight, try acknowledging their efforts—*and* someone else's. If you repeatedly make the effort to include the quieter members of your team in the conversation, you'll eventually improve the dynamics.

Show and tell. Just like *The Ghost*, *The Pretender* may not be aware she's coming across as larger than life. Offer to videotape her giving a presentation or doing a mock debrief about a project she's been working on. If she sees how she comes across to others, she's more likely to take ownership of her behavior and make lasting changes.

Ask unexpected questions. If your colleague strikes you as over-rehearsed, try asking some questions to get him to look at things from another angle. Your goal is not to trip him up or embarrass him—just to get him to be real. If he gets positive feedback for speaking more honestly and thoughtfully, he may adopt this as a new style. We repeat what we're rewarded for.

From Star to Sherpa

When I asked Antonio how he wanted people to experience him, he scratched his head and adjusted his glasses. He was reflecting. Finally, he replied, "I want to be seen as a mountain climber, taking my team to the summit. There will be twists and turns. But I've got their backs and I'll help lead them to the top."

"So—are you saying that you want to be a business Sherpa?" I asked.

He agreed enthusiastically—but then realized that if he wanted his team to follow him on the climb, he had to tone down his outer presence and make them feel more involved and valued.

First, he started giving his team more positive feedback. He'd previously been so focused on zooming ahead to whatever was next that he'd neglected to celebrate his team's victories. He also started bringing members of his team along to board meetings in order to share the credit for their successes. Additionally, he made an effort to introduce one message at a time, instead of leaping from peak to peak so quickly.

Antonio has made huge strides. People are responding far better to him, and he's earning buy-in from his team. He's on his way to becoming a Sherpa instead of a solo climber.

....

AN OUTER PRESENCE HEROINE

A young teen from Maine, ticked off by flagrant Photoshopping in magazines, spun her criticism into a crusade. As a result, she led an influential, industry-altering outer-presence crusade.

Fourteen-year-old Julia Bluhm started a petition on Change.org against altered photos in *Seventeen* magazine. Within days, her petition had more than 84,000 supporters. Within a month, Julia and her mom were invited to New York to meet with *Seventeen's* editor-in-chief. And now the magazine has made a commitment to change.

Seventeen calls the truce a "Body Peace Treaty." Starting with its August 2012 issue, the magazine promised not to doctor girls' body or face shapes. It also vowed to share raw images from photo shoots on the magazine's Tumblr blog so readers can follow how the photos are retouched during the editing process.

It's no secret that teenagers have long been influenced by images they see in the media. The magazine industry has been split on the subject of excessive retouching. And while it might not seem like an earth-shattering topic, the issues of truth, transparency, and the delicate self-image of developing young women are at stake.

This issue may affect a young woman in your life. I know it affected me when I was a teen. Growing up in rural Indiana, a *Seventeen* magazine from the local grocery store was a monthly treat. I bought into the notion that the models on the pages were perfect and that the image in my mirror did not measure up. As a small-town girl with no business acumen, I was too naïve to realize that the images were manipulated by big city publishers.

There are two key influencers at play here:

1. 14-year-old Julia
2. You.

Julia's role is obvious. Her crusade led a magazine to change its policy. Your role may not seem so clear—but you have an equal opportunity to influence others in your daily life.

....

10 TIPS TO CENTER YOUR OUTER PRESENCE

1. **Recognize that one size doesn't fit all.** Adapt to each audience. Make it your mission to help others feel that you're centered on them—because you *are*.

2. **Let people in.** Allow others to see that you're fully human. Don't hide every flaw; your humanity is a powerful tool.

3. **Listen on purpose.** Listening and asking perceptive questions makes people feel respected and understood.

4. **Look like you care.** Learn how to smile honestly to warm up your face. The psychological principle of reciprocation will kick in.

5. **Find your voice.** Breathe deeply from your diaphragm so your voice is resonant and doesn't sound too high or strained.

6. **Don't sound scripted.** Prepare, but don't *over*prepare. Keep a spark of life in your words so people feel your passion and compassion.

7. **Be quick to praise.** Acknowledge others' efforts and always remember to include quieter members of your team. You'll help people feel included and improve group dynamics.

8. **Don't let your appearance distract from your message.** Dress appropriately, professionally, and simply. Exude confidence and approachability.

9. **Be a great wingman.** Support your colleagues when they make good points. It'll encourage

them to speak up, and it will boost your own presence.

10. **Quiet your lower body.** Do you pace back and forth when you're at the front of the room, or bounce your legs when you're seated? Calm your happy feet. You'll gain power and presence.

Identify the top three conditions that tend to knock your outer presence off-center:

Outer Presence Action Plan

1. _____

_____

2. _____

_____

3. _____

_____

Three ways you plan to keep yourself centered in these situations:

1. _____

_____

2. _____

_____

3. _____

_____

Bringing It All Together
Becoming the Real Deal

Sooner or later, we all reach that defining moment when the lightning bolt of reality strikes: we grasp that *our ideal must give way to what's real.*

It's a liberating realization. At last, you give yourself permission to stop the masquerade. You no longer try to be that "ideal" person that either you or societal pressures have built up in your head—the person preventing you from living your most significant, meaningful life. For some, that moment comes early. For others, it's an end-of-life revelation.

I'm asking you to become the real deal *now* rather than later. *Now*—to earn trust. *Now*—to elevate performance. *Now*—to interface beautifully with the world.

As you discovered throughout this book, each Layer of Presence—Inner, Outer, and Verbal— can be like a seesaw, teetering back and forth.

If you're off-center, you can pay a substantial price.

So I'll ask you the same question I did when you started reading this book: are you the *real deal?*

You are.

I realize you've just discovered things that you may want to improve upon. Maybe you feel like you've got your work cut out for you—as though you're miles away from becoming the centered, authentic, purpose-driven leader you aspire to be.

But that doesn't change my answer. You *are* the real deal. You always have been.

Think about the moments when you do show up as the authentic you. Maybe it's at home with people you love, or at lunch with your oldest friends, or at your place of worship. Maybe you're the real deal at work—some of the time, with some of your colleagues.

Integerate all three layers

See, you *can* be the real deal. You've already spent a portion of your life being centered. The work ahead is to bring that authenticity into all three layers of your being: Inner, Outer, and Verbal.

I know that isn't as simple as it sounds. The kind of work I've been talking about takes courage and dedication.

I know—because I've experienced this firsthand. For years, caution was my default approach to life. I spent far too long showing up as less than myself in all three layers. I didn't want to upset or offend anyone, so I held parts of myself back, stayed silent when I should have spoken up, or put on a front to mask my true feelings. I feared criticism and did everything I could be neutral, thinking that would make me bulletproof. Of course, I later realized there's *no such thing* as bulletproof. Humanity is your best asset.

Perhaps you're unconsciously reliving old patterns from childhood or adolescence, too. I promise you, finding the courage to break the pattern and start showing up as the real deal is liberating and worth the effort.

Embracing the audacity to face my fears and get real transformed me personally as well as professionally. The same thing will happen to you when you let yourself start showing up as the real you.

Are you ready to start down the proven path to influence and executive presence? Here's a quick review of what it takes to become the real deal.

Layer One: Inner Presence

The real deal starts within. Everything flows from here. Maybe you get anxious or are ruled by pride.

If you're a perfectionist, change your mind-set. Seek excellence, not perfection. If you're *The Worrier*, worry well—and then move on. If you're *The Egotist*, get off your high horse (I couldn't resist that old saying from my dad) and learn to stop deflecting blame and creating shame.

A crucial truth about inner presence is that focusing on yourself is counterproductive. It prevents you from connecting with others. To stay centered, live your values and stay focused on a purpose greater than yourself.

Layer Two: Verbal Presence

Your efforts to ensure that people are willing to listen to you are wasted if you don't have something useful to say. Are you *The Mouse*? Learn how and when to contribute. Are you *The Motor Mouth*? Listening is the desire to hear. Hit your mute button once in a while to hear others' perspectives.

Centering your Verbal Presence turns rhetoric into results. Start by identifying your ideal outcome, and then tailor your message to your listener's needs. Be on point. You'll start crafting messages that resonate with others and as a result, they'll pay attention to you face-to-face. They'll respond to your e-mails and voice messages. They won't be able to ignore you.

....

Layer Three: Outer Presence

We all want people to find us credible and likable. But our intentions and our impact often are disconnected. If you're *The Ghost*, step out of the background. If you're *The Pretender*, dial back that false front. Identify the people or situations that throw your outer presence off-center. Maybe you aren't aware how your facial, vocal, or body energies are affecting others. Ask. Listen. Videotape yourself, even, to see yourself as others do. Seek feedback from people you trust. Discovering how you come across to the world gives you the opportunity to transform the way people respond to you.

....

All of this takes effort. But you'll gain influence and executive presence. The real deal is inside of you, just waiting to show up in *every* situation.

Your *clients* want you to be the real deal.

Your *colleagues* want you to be the real deal.

Most important, *you* want to be the real deal.

I hope you're inspired to be the whole person you're meant to be.

Embrace it. Live it. Every day.

Acknowledgments

It takes a remarkable team of real people to write a book about being *the real deal*. Every person whose name you're about to read embodies the centered qualities that you just finished reading about.

A remarkable team of real people

To my writing team: Sarah Morgan, who made me a better writer by helping me bring my coaching experiences to life. Sarah helped me communicate in print the way that I do in person. In the early stages of this project, Allison Nazarian also helped me organize my thoughts.

To my publishing team: Wiley's business publisher and vice president Matt Holt, who believed in me and prodded me to write about lessons learned from my coaching experiences. My editor, Lauren Murphy, has had my back, encouraging me, and gently nudging me to stay on track despite my hectic schedule. Development editor, Christine Moore, provided valuable feedback on the manuscript as it trickled in, chapter-by-chapter. Michael Freeland provided the clever cover design for both this book and *Talk Less, Say More*. Lauren Freestone guided me through the editing and layout process. (If you're a writer, you know how crucial all of these stages are to a book's success.)

To my business partners and contributors: Marshall Goldsmith, who wrote the foreword. I believe Marshall is the gold standard in executive coaching and I'm incredibly honored that he shared his thoughts about *Become the Real Deal* with you. Andrew Sobel and Bob Burg, my beloved friends who read the manuscript and shared their advice and wisdom. Nick Morgan, who provided expert guidance with the book's title and helped me develop the keynote speech that accompanies this book. Kevin Small led the title and cover efforts of the book that's in your hands. Amanda Brown thoughtfully filtered through more than a decade's worth of my research, assimilated it, and boiled down more than 3,500 people's responses to their critical essence. Sara Alvarado, in my office, kept track of all of the research over the years and also kept the business running smoothly as I was hunkered down writing this book. Alan Baker and Beth Kuchar of Rapture Studio, and Jana Vanadia and Ryan Shull of Studio Think, who helped bring the book's concepts to life with terrific graphics. Mark Hamer, who masterfully created the videos that bring the material to life both in the keynote speech and the book's digital version. And Eric Mull, who shot my author photograph, keeping it natural and real.

To my family, who infuse my life with purpose and perspective: Ali, Spencer, Christine, Mike, Dad, Doug and our newest edition, little Diesel—thank you for keeping me grounded and teaching me life lessons to keep it real. If you read the dedication, you already discovered my inspiration—my late mother, Joan, whose life was cut short, but whose humanity and presence is still felt as the real deal.

I'm so grateful   *And finally, to my extraordinary clients*: It is an honor to serve you. I gain wisdom from you each and every day—you're teaching me much more than I could ever teach you.

I'm so grateful to have all of you in my life.

About the Author

Connie Dieken is an executive coach and advisor to the upper echelon of senior executives at some of the world's biggest brands. She helps skyrocket senior leaders to their highest performance by transforming them into true influencers who are the real deal. She's helped  thousands of leaders from organizations such as Nestlé, eBay, Apple, Olympus, American Greetings, The Cleveland Clinic, and McDonald's achieve successful results.

She is also an insightful keynote speaker who delivers high-content, high-energy programs at major conferences and events around the globe. She weaves her coaching adventures with ripped-from-the-headlines leadership stories that help audiences achieve their highest potential. Her current leadership and sales topics include Become the Real Deal; Talk Less, Say More; and The Influential Presenter.

She's the author of the bestseller, *Talk Less, Say More: 3 Habits to Influence Others and Make Things Happen*, she's a weekly contributor to The Huffington Post, and she's also been featured in *The Wall Street Journal, USA Today, CNBC, The Los Angeles Times, The Chicago Tribune, Men's Health, Women's Day*, and *Crain's Business*.

Before launching her coaching firm in 2000, Connie was a television anchorwoman, reporter, and producer. During her broadcasting career, she won five Emmy awards and a Telly award and was inducted into the Radio/Television Broadcasters Hall of Fame.

She has also represented more than 50 companies as their spokesperson, including Intel, Sealy, GE, and Goodyear.

A rotten cook and bowler, she instead gets her kicks out by helping to develop others' leadership talents.

Index